# THE ANGELINA PROJECT

DRAMA SERIES 19

Canadä

Guernica Editions Inc. acknowledges the support of
The Canada Council for the Arts.
Guernica Editions Inc. acknowledges the support of
the Ontario Arts Council.
Guernica Editions Inc. acknowledges the financial support of the
Government of Canada through the Book Publishing Industry
Development Program (BPIDP).

FRANK CANINO

# THE ANGELINA PROJECT

A Play In Two Acts

GUERNICA
TORONTO·BUFFALO·LANCASTER (U.K.)
2000

Antonio D'Alfonso, editor
Guernica Editions Inc.
P.O. Box 117, Station P, Toronto (ON), Canada M5S 2S6
2250 Military Road, Tonawanda, N.Y. 14150-6000 U.S.A.
Gazelle, Falcon House, Queen Square, Lancaster LA1 1RN U.K.

Typeset by Selina.
Printed in Canada.

Legal Deposit — Second Quarter
National Library of Canada
Library of Congress Catalog Card Number: 00-101693

Canadian Cataloguing in Publication Data
Canino, Frank
The Angelina project
(Drama series ; 19)
Included some text in Italian.
ISBN 1-55071-109-1
I. Titles. II. Series.
PS8555.A55453A76   2000   C812'.6   C00-900635-4
PR9199.5.C295A76   2000

# Contents

## From the Playwright's Notes

What *The Angelina Project* isn't.
NOT a documentary,
NOT an historical/ethnic recreation,
NOT a kitchen sink drama,
NOT a New Age psycho-soap opera about victims and abuse.

What it is (maybe).
A mosaic in which bits and pieces of past and present start to hang together. A time and place fantasia that begins chaotically and arrives at some order and understanding. Remember Amelia's speech: "There's no such thing as the past being over. It keeps happening again and again — right here and now."
Something closer to a film — or a dream.

Or it may be about
Being caught between generations and cultures,
Beginning with one conscious objective but accomplishing something different,
Finding out how family secrets and lies have shaped your personality.

# Some Historical Background

"On the afternoon of Easter Sunday, 16 April 1911, Angelina Napolitano, a twenty-eight-year-old Italian mother of four, killed her husband with an axe as he lay asleep in the bedroom of the quarters they rented in Sault Ste. Marie, Ontario. This is the bare-bones opening of an article, 'Murder, Womanly Virtue and Motherhood' by Karen Dubinsky and Franca Iacovetta" *(The Canadian Historical Review,* Vol. 72, No. 4, December 1991).

In late 1994 producer Diane Quinn brought me this article because she thought the material had theatrical possibilities. She set no limitations other than there could be no more than eight actors, and that she preferred a text that was verbally and visually imaginative. As I researched the story, I developed a semi-fictional approach in which the effects of Angelina's actions would be traced through the following generations of her family. The script went through several drafts under such worthy writers as Paul Quarrington, Sharon Pollock, Romulus Linney and finally dramaturge Elise Dewsberry, in November of 1998, when we did a four day workshop that eventuated in a reading at Théâtre Passe Muraille's Backspace.

By this time I was well into draft eight, and was heartily desperate to finish the script forever. There had been several readings previous to November, 1998. Everyone had a different take on the material. Everyone found different problems with it, even after it won several awards.

"It's really a novel," said a poet.

"It's not readable!" insisted a dramaturge from New York.

"The script makes no sense in this fragmented structure," said an actor (who later reversed the opinion when he heard it read aloud — a pattern that became very common over the next three years).

I continued writing and revising and simplifying and editing and adding. This script is the result. It has been a long journey in which I unintentionally rediscovered my Italian heritage. "Why don't you have any Italian friends?" my Aunt Rose would demand, as I was growing up. Because — I think now — I had no idea of Angelina Napolitano's story — or even the brave but dark story of my own family.

This play is for anyone who is finding his way down the same road.

"There's no such thing as the past being over. It keeps happening again and again — right here and now."

# THE ANGELINA PROJECT

*For Angelina Restivo-Canino, 1908-1987*

TIME AND PLACE
The present: just before Easter, in Toronto.
The past: over several years in Sault Ste. Marie, North Bay and Kingston.

SETTING
Open space with several swivel chairs or stools. Two defined areas: Amelia's computer desk surrounded by office clutter, and Raffaella's kitchen table, covered with cooking ingredients. A large chair upstage for Angelina.

CHARACTER-ACTOR BREAKDOWN
The Women of the Family:
Angelina Napolitano/Queen Clytemnestra
Raffaella Bortolato
Amelia Covello
Toni Covello
Other Family Members and the People of their World:
Woman #1: Elisabeth Bewley; Defense Lawyer McFadden
Woman #2: Aunt Rosa, Effie MacIssac, Carole, Francine Thompson, Angelina's mother, Anna Fishback
Man # 1: Pietro Napolitano, Vinny Covello, Hughie McDonald, Constable White
Man #2: Don Sedgwick, Fr. Finegan, Prosecutor Meredith, Dr. Gimby, Photographer, Editor Curran
Cast: Judge Britton

# ACT ONE

## Shift 1

*Pin spot on Amelia. She sips a drink and closes her eyes, rocking back and forth.*

**AMELIA**
*Solo.*

I dream of a woman, sitting in a small room. No doors. One square window high up. No sound. She gets up, walks around, faster and faster, looking for a way to escape. She jumps up to the window, but it's too high. She's running in desperation, panting and sweating with the burden of her clothes and her swollen belly. She's gasping for air. When suddenly — *miracolo!* — there's an axe in her hands! O gift from the gods! O sign from heaven! And she lifts it high and begins to cut her way out, smashing through the walls — out. Out. OUT.

*Behind her appears the actress playing Angelina/Clytemnestra with a huge cape that she drapes around herself and Amelia.*

**ANGELINA AND AMELIA**

Quick! Give me an axe! I will cut down Agamemnon and any who stand in my way!

*Angelina starts to recite the text of Clytemnestra in Italian with Amelia echoing her.*

**CLYTEMNESTRA**
*Tu mi assecondi?*

**AMELIA**
*Overlapping her.*
Are you my judge?

ANGELINA
*Sei disposto?*

AMELIA
My jury?

ANGELINA
*Mi critichi?*

AMELIA
Will you have me exiled? Cursed?

ANGELINA
*È lo stesso.*

AMELIA
The score is even.

ANGELINA
*Ecco Agamennone! Sì, mio marito.*

AMELIA
Here lies Agamemnon who was my husband.

ANGELINA
*Morto! Colpo di questa abile mano.*

AMELIA
Slain by this cunning hand of mine.

ANGELINA
*Autrice di vendetta.*

AMELIA
I, the queen of vengeance.

ANGELINA
*Questi i fatti.*

AMELIA
And I have done well.

*On the soundtrack, Andrea Bocelli singing "Con te partirò."*
*Amelia takes another drink and resumes work at her computer,*
*obviously stressed out. Lights up on the rest of the cast who*
*enter with furniture and props. While they place them in*
*position, they whisper-chant the following couplet continu-*
*ously, as they taunt Amelia with their speeches.*

THE GROUP
Testify. Accuse. Confess.
Lie. Withhold. Just plain guess.

MAN #1
*Overlapping.*
If I find you in the house, I will kill you and that fucking baby
in your stomach.

ANGELINA
*Overlapping.*
I told him, I could never do that. I would rather die first.

MAN #2
*Overlapping.*
The doctor says there were seven wounds. And even more!

RAFFAELLA
*Overlapping.*
Every family has its secrets. Ours were worse than others,
that's all.

AMELIA
What do you want me to do? I feel inadequate and stupid
and . . .
　　　*The speeches overlap faster and faster, blurring into a jumble*
　　　*of sound, while Amelia protests louder and louder. The Bocelli*
　　　*song becomes woozy and distorted.*

WOMAN #2

The world needs noble martyrs, like Mrs. Napolitano, to lift it out of the foul rut of immorality — a fate far worse than murder.

MAN #1

I give you lots of trouble, and make you go far away. But any place you go, I find you and kill you!

ANGELINA

He say he will take my children away.

AMELIA

*Shouting over them.*

I keep trying harder and harder. But it's never enough!

RAFFAELLA

What good is the truth? Especially for a child.

ANGELINA

I did not know what to do, and I was near crazy.

RAFFAELLA

A liar and a thief — is that what you've become, young lady?

AMELIA

Mama, I'm not a whore because I stay out after midnight.

*Screaming over them.*

I'm doing the best that I can! Mama, it's the best I can do!

*The distorted music abruptly cuts out. The actors scatter, sit in their chairs around the area. Amelia sits at her computer, pours herself another shot of grappa and starts to key in some material. Meanwhile, Raffaella works imperturbably at her table.*

## Shift 2

*Distorted sound of gavel banging, as lights come up on the cast facing us.*

### JUSTICE BRITTON

Angelina Napolitano, the sentence of the court is that you be taken hence to the gaol until Wednesday, the ninth day of August next, that you be taken from the gaol to the place of execution and that you be there hanged by the neck until you are dead. And may God have mercy on your soul.

### ANGELINA

Here I am. Take me. I am ready to die.

## Shift 3

*Phone ring. Lights on Woman#2 as Carole.*

### CAROLE

Paraphrase and summary don't make for good research. All these references to old Italian plays are useless. And why are you bringing in figures like Clytemnestra?

### AMELIA

I had all this material from my undergrad thesis, and I wanted to draw a parallel between —

### CAROLE

*Cutting her off sharply.*

Baby, you are in the real world now. This is a Master's program — for grown-ups! Forget mythology. Forget poetry. Above all, forget theatre. You're supposed to be analyzing how the law treats women.

### AMELIA

Carole, I'm doing the best I can!

*Drinking again.*

Between you and her, I need a lawyer.

## Shift 4

*Phone rings as lights come up on Woman #1 as Elisabeth. She rifles through an attaché case and takes off her lawyer's robes.*

ELISABETH
O'Connor, Goldberg, Pantalone and Bewley. Ms. Bewley speaking.

AMELIA
Elisabeth, it's Amelia. How are you doing?

ELISABETH
Just got back from court. What about you?

AMELIA
I've got my mother on my back about all the cooking we have to do for Easter. Then Carole's on my case about the thesis. I've got tons of research, but there's this one case. It's like I'm fixated on it. I feel inadequate and stupid and . . .

ELISABETH
*Overlapping.*
Don't let the Dragon Lady get to you.

AMELIA
But if I flunk out what will I do?

ELISABETH
You are going to finish the goddam thesis and get that degree — and a new man.

AMELIA
Plus Vinny and Toni are driving me nuts.

ELISABETH
Be happy you have a family.

AMELIA
Are you spending the holidays with your mother?

ELISABETH
Not if Cheryl isn't invited.

AMELIA
Listen. The Bortolatos and the Covellos are sharing their Easter dinner. Why don't you join us?

ELISABETH
*Teasing.*
Oh honey, a couple of dozen wops and two dykes? Uh-uh! No one would stay for dessert.

AMELIA
*Humorously exasperated.*
Stop that! I need help . . . now!

ELISABETH
I'll be there in half an hour. With food.

## Shift 5

*A distorted banging of the gavel as lights come up on Man #2 as Dr. Gimby in the witness chair. Elisabeth rises and moves into his area as Defense Lawyer McFadden.*

DR. GIMBY
In the High Court of Justice: Rex versus Angelina Napolitano. Tried at Sault Ste. Marie, Monday, May 8, in the year of Our Lord, 1932. Archibald McFadden for the Defense.

MCFADDEN
With your Honor's permission, I would like to cross-examine the witness.

JUSTICE BRITTON
Yes, Mr. McFadden. Please proceed.

MCFADDEN
Dr. Gimby, could you tell from the body how long Pietro Napolitano had been dead?

DR. GIMBY
Rigor mortis was starting to set in. I should think two or three hours. Mr. Napolitano was lying in bed on his left side. His knees were drawn up and there were wounds on his head.

MCFADDEN
Were these wounds sufficient to cause death?

DR. GIMBY
Yes. I would judge that he had received three blows.

AMELIA
No, wait! Somewhere else it says seven.

MCFADDEN
The coroner insists there were seven or more wounds. But three would have been sufficient to kill him?

DR. GIMBY
In my professional opinion, yes.

MCFADDEN
Even if a person of no great size or strength were wielding the axe.

DR. GIMBY
Absolutely.

AMELIA
They can't even get the number right!
        *Looking through files.*
Where is it?

MCFADDEN

So seven blows or more would indicate the murderer was not acting with cold calculation. In fact, was striking out in anger or fear.

## *Shift 6*

*Phone rings. Lights on Man#2 as Don Sedwick.*

DON

Amelia? You there? I really have to talk to you.

AMELIA

Don, I asked you not to call me at home.

DON

Look, I know you're upset. But about last weekend —

AMELIA

Oh Don, please. I can't deal with this now.

DON

I'm sorry if I pressured you into . . .

AMELIA

I just didn't plan for it to happen that way.

DON

I'm happy it did. But not if it makes you feel guilty.

AMELIA

I am going crazy with my thesis and the holidays and —

DON

I don't want to make things worse for you. But I can't bear to lose you.

AMELIA

Not now. Please give me a little space.

DON
As long as I know I'll see you again.

AMELIA
*Hanging up.*
Please go away.

## Shift 7

PROSECUTOR MEREDITH
Mrs. Napolitano, you told your husband that you and Nish slept together?

ANGELINA
As long as I get the money, it was all right with him.

MEREDITH
And you were two months pregnant when you had this relationship with Mr. Nish?

ANGELINA
Yes, sir.

MEREDITH
This was in November when the Children's Aid Society was going to take your children away from you, because —

ANGELINA
No! No true! They try, but is all lies.

MEREDITH
Your neighbors said your children were going hungry and asking them for food. That you were an unfit mother with a man living in your house while your husband went away to look for work.

ANGELINA
No. Mr Nish is my . . . *come se dice: bordante?*

MCFADDEN
A boarder, your Honor.

ANGELINA
*Sì.* When Pietro leave, he no say when he come back. Gone so many weeks . . . no money left, so I take in a boarder. Mr. Nish very nice. Very quiet. Very clean. Help me to cut wood, play with the children. He eat with us, and we talk. I am so alone. I not know if my husband come back, and this man is good to us all. But we were only together for one week. Then my husband come home and hit him, so he run away. And Pietro beat me so bad —

MEREDITH
But your children also had bruises on their bodies, which they told their teacher *you* inflicted on them.

ANGELINA
Sometimes I feel crazy with all the noise . . . and the baby inside me . . . and no money from my husband . . .

MEREDITH
So you did strike your own children?

AMELIA
*Rushing to her defense.*
Sometimes one kid can drive you crazy, much less four — you smug Anglo-Saxon fuck!
*But she is pulled back into the present with an unexpected visitor.*

## *Shift 8*

ZIA ROSA
Amelia *cara,* I bring you the ricotta for the cannoles.

AMELIA
Aunt Rosa, I'm in the middle of working and I have to finish
soon.

ZIA ROSA
You have to use *cioccolato nero. Come si chiama?* [Dark chocolate. How do you say that?]

AMELIA
Dark chocolate. My mother's going to do the cannoles.

ZIA ROSA
*Gesù Maria! Son stanca.* [Jesus, Mary! I'm tired.]

AMELIA
You want some coffee?

ZIA ROSA
*Madonna! Che succede a tua madre? È pazza?* [What's wrong
with your mother? Is she crazy?]

AMELIA
Aunt Rosa, I'm so tired. English, please.

ZIA ROSA
I think you gonna do all the desserts.

AMELIA
No, no, no. The Covellos bring the *braciole;* the Bortolatos
bring pastas. That means your lasagna too, of course. Mama
does the desserts.

ZIA ROSA
You and Toni help her?

AMELIA
As much as we can.

ZIA ROSA
Toni has a *fidanzato* yet?

AMELIA
No, no serious boyfriend.

ZIA ROSA
Madonna! At her age I had two kids already.

AMELIA
Girls marry late nowadays, Aunt Rosa.

ZIA ROSA
*Sono tutte puttane.*   [They're all whores.] You graduate soon?

AMELIA
If I finish my thesis.

ZIA ROSA
Theee-sees? *Ma che cos'è?*  [But what is that?]

AMELIA
I got something burning on the stove!

## *Shift 9*

*Distorted banging of a gavel, as lights come up on the witness area.*

DEFENSE LAWYER MCFADDEN
Mrs. Napolitano, let us go to the time you had a serious quarrel last year. When was that?

ANGELINA
On the 20 November. Sunday morning.

MCFADDEN
What did he do to you on that occasion?

ANGELINA
He start to fight me. He cut me all over. Like my face . . . here.
*As she touches her face, McFadden pauses to let that image of her scarred face sink in.*

MCFADDEN
Did you strike back at him?

ANGELINA
No.

MCFADDEN
After he stabbed you, where did you go?

ANGELINA
In hospital.

MCFADDEN
But where were you found before that?

ANGELINA
I go to run away. To river.

MCFADDEN
To kill yourself?

ANGELINA
Yes.

MCFADDEN
Now, please tell us what happened on the morning of Easter Sunday.

ANGELINA
My husband come home that morning. He fight with me. He want me to be a bad woman. He say . . .

*Man #1 has appeared behind her and lifts her up in a headlock, so she is paralyzed in his arms. He is drunk but quietly threatening.*

PIETRO
If you no get thirty dollars, I kill you. We have rent to pay. If we no have enough money, we lose the house. You got any money this morning?

ANGELINA
No, I have no money at all.

PIETRO
I go to bed now. When I wake up, if you in the house with no money, I kill you. No. I take away your babies!
*He drops her into the chair and walks away quickly.*

MCFADDEN
How long did this quarrel last?

ANGELINA
All the morning.

MCFADDEN
Mrs. Napolitano, can you tell me what frame of mind you were in when your husband went to bed?

ANGELINA
I was feeling sorry at what he say, that he want to take the children away. And I start to cry and think I don't know what I am going to do. I have no friends or nothing at all. All my family back in Italy. I did not know what to do, and I was near crazy.

MCFADDEN
You felt crazy! In what condition are you now?

ANGELINA
On the 26 of this month, I am seven months in the family way.

MCFADDEN
And the father of this child was Pietro Napolitano?

ANGELINA
Only he could be the father. On my honor.

## Shift 10

CAROLE

You're supposed to be writing about the treatment of women by the justice system. You keep confusing the political issue with ethnic problems. Stop fixating on this Napolitano case. I want to know how all kinds of women were treated in a courtroom when they broke the law. So you need to compare many cases. I am looking for cold facts and analysis. *Not* literature. *Not* ethnicity! So don't get lost in the lasagna!

## Shift 11

AMELIA

*After another drink.*

All right, all right, all right, all right! Here goes, Dragon Lady.
*Reading.*

"In fiction and in fact, the situation is the same: the legal system was created by men and for men. When women were given the vote, they were not automatically allowed to run for office. In Quebec a woman could not practice law until 1942, while most provinces did not allow women to serve on juries until 1945."

*Starting to key text into computer.*

So a woman in a courtroom two generations ago — in Ontario or elsewhere — was a misfit. The law would neither acknowledge nor . . .

*Pausing as she tries to figure out the spelling.*

Jesus, Mary . . . acknowledge . . . do you use a "k" or a "c"?
*Shaking her head and continuing. But she stops suddenly as the system freezes. She frantically hits several keys to no avail and loses control of herself.*

No, don't do that!

*She howls in frustration. Toni enters with groceries.*

TONI

What's wrong now?

AMELIA
This goddam computer is crashing again!

TONI
All you have to do is . . .
*Turning the system off then back on.*
Did you save your work from this morning?

AMELIA
Yes . . . no . . . maybe. I was going to be late for class and the
phone was going crazy, so I just ran out. Ouch!
*Pressing hands against her eyes as if in pain.*

TONI
I have those Tylenol 3s if you want some.

AMELIA
I used them up already. Can you get more?

TONI
They're prescription, ma.

AMELIA
*Quietly desperate.*
I need them.

TONI
Here's your file coming up . . . just as you left it.

AMELIA
Jesus, Mary and Joseph.

TONI
No, just Toni Covello. Computer geek.

AMELIA
Don't get smart. Can I work now?

TONI
All yours.

*Getting up. With pointed sarcasm.*
And you're welcome.

### AMELIA
Thank you! Except you forgot to turn on the crock pot, so there's no minestrone for dinner.

### TONI
There's leftover lasagna in the freezer. I'll put it in the micro-wave.

### AMELIA
Plus you forgot the laundry.

### TONI
*Showing laundry cart.*
Here we are.

### AMELIA
It's not folded.

### TONI
Ok, ok. How about some music?
*Amelia shrugs and continues working, as Toni turns on a recording of Bocelli singing and starts to fold items.*
How's the work going?

### AMELIA
I don't think I'm good at this kind of material.

### TONI
Bullshit! You did fine at York.

### AMELIA
In Italian literature, where I was comfortable. But I'm no good at this research and political analysis — dammit!

### TONI
What's wrong now?

AMELIA
I want to cut and paste this section but . . .

TONI
Here.
*Showing her.*

AMELIA
Are you going out with Jorge tonight?

TONI
Yeah. I'm playing at Cameron House. I'm taking the car.

AMELIA
You just make sure that Pablo Picasso doesn't drive my car.

TONI
He's from El Salvador.

AMELIA
Wherever. He'll have you barefoot and pregnant, cleaning his paintbrushes.

TONI
And he's a sculptor.

AMELIA
So he'll slice you up.

TONI
Ma, it could be worse: he could be Portuguese.

AMELIA
Stop that!

TONI
Then, for chrissakes, get a life and leave me alone. I have to rehearse with the band. John Alcorn's pianist got sick, so I'm doing backup.

AMELIA

More screwing around on Queen West.

TONI

No, it's a job. Money! *Capisci?* [Understand?] And I am going to move in with Peter and Mark.

AMELIA

Your father's going to kill you. You can't live with a bunch of . . .

> *Catching herself before she uses the politically incorrect term "faggots."*

TONI

> *Taunting her.*

Faggots? At least I'm safe with them.

> *Mocking.*

What about your "Miss Melanzana"?

AMELIA

Elisabeth is different! She was my maid of honor! And my best friend at school.

TONI

Listen. You can be a hip feminist *or* Mrs. "Mamma Mia" Covello in the kitchen. Just choose!

AMELIA

I hate it when you're like this. I could put a knife through your heart.

TONI

Keep it Italian, Mama. Make that a stiletto.

> *Finishing at the computer, as she turns back to Amelia.*

There. You'll be fine. Gotta dress.

AMELIA

Your father's gonna break your neck. If you move out, it's like you're dead!

TONI
And you should have the guts to walk out and start something new. If you really like this Don guy . . .

AMELIA
That's enough.

TONI
Papa is too busy fucking his Polish girlfriend . . .

AMELIA
*Basta!*

TONI
. . . To worry about us. Him and La Polacca are ——

AMELIA
*Slapping her.*
Shut up!

TONI
*Long pause, then deliberately cold.*
I have to go to rehearsal.

AMELIA
O Jesus, honey, I'm sorry. I . . .


## *Shift 12*

*On the sound track, the Bocelli song abruptly crosscuts with a burst of Italian opera . . . perhaps Puccini's* Tosca, *Act 2. Lights cross fade to Raffaella who is busy rolling dough and listening to a radio broadcast at high volume. She talks over her speaker-phone.*

RAFFAELLA
Amelia! If I'm ever gonna get those cannoles made, I need the ricotta now.

AMELIA
Zia Rosa just came with it, Mama. Can you wait till tomorrow? And can you turn that damn music down!

RAFFAELLA
Tomorrow we have to shop and clean. I want to go to church
on Good Friday. So the more I do now the better it is.

AMELIA
*Overlapping.*
Ok, ok! I'm just going crazy with my thesis.

RAFFAELLA
Why can't Toni bring the stuff over?

AMELIA
She's got a rehearsal.

RAFFAELLA
When she should be helping you. What kind of daughter are
you raisin'?

AMELIA
*Interrupting.*
Ma, I don't need this now!

RAFFAELLA
I need help if we're feeding all the Bortolatos and Covellos
on Sunday.

AMELIA
Maybe Vinny can bring it over.

RAFFAELLA
*Pause, then the final jab.*
Don't forget the chocolate chips.

AMELIA
Mama, I'm doing the best that I can do!

## *Shift 13*

*Music cuts out abruptly. Man #1, playing Vinny, Amelia's husband, walks up to her.*

**VINNY**
Amelia, where the fuck are my diamond cufflinks?

**AMELIA**
In the lacquer box under your shirts. Can you take the ricotta to my mother's?

**VINNY**
I'm running late.

**AMELIA**
Why aren't you eating at home?

**VINNY**
It's business, ok? With some guys from out of town.

**AMELIA**
All right. But I want you to talk to Toni.

**VINNY**
What's wrong with her?

**AMELIA**
She wants to move out.

**VINNY**
With that Spic boyfriend?

**AMELIA**
Those guys on Queen West.

**VINNY**
Faggots? *Stu cazz'!* [My balls!] What are you doin' to her?

**AMELIA**
Why is it my fault?

VINNY

Because you're too busy at school to pay any attention to us. Or running off to Italy or to some goddam women's group.

AMELIA

Maybe I should just be out of here for good.

VINNY

Yeah, yeah. I'll believe it when I see it.

AMELIA

If I get a lawyer, I know that I can get my share, plus alimony.

VINNY

Do you know how much he's gonna take you for? Because, believe me, I'll drag it out as long as I can. You'll take your ass out of here and nothing else.

AMELIA

Why are you doing this to me?

VINNY

You fuck me and I'll fuck you right back.

AMELIA

I swear to God, I hate you so much I could —

VINNY

Go fuck yourself!

## *Shift 14*

*The music from Tosca returns. Amelia walks into Raffaela's kitchen area.*

AMELIA

Mama, I wanted to kill him.

RAFFAELLA

I don't see any bruises on you.

AMELIA

There are other ways to hurt people. What's truly ridiculous is I'm even afraid of what Vinny will think of me, if I divorce him.

RAFFAELLA

Your friends and neighbors will only be worse. And don't expect any help from me.

AMELIA

Vinny will have to pay me something.

RAFFAELLA

You've been living on more than "something" for the last twenty years. All those trips to Europe. Sending you back to university. Whatever else he is, he's generous.

AMELIA

So he can show off me and Toni in our name-brand clothes and cars. It's about his pride, Mama.

RAFFAELLA

He can't keep his pants zipped. That's all. If that's the worst you have to put up with . . .

AMELIA
*Cutting her off.*
Why do you want me to hang on to Vinny so badly?

RAFFAELLA

You'll be worse off without him. How often has he lifted a hand to you? In my day, you had to have a black eye or a broken arm to prove a man was bad to you. A slap or a punch didn't count.

AMELIA

I swore I would never raise my hand to Toni, or to him, no matter what.

RAFFAELLA
You don't have a choice sometimes.

AMELIA
No. I won't believe that. Especially after what my own father did to me. And to you, Mama.

RAFFAELLA
Hughie was all right, except when he was drunk out of his mind.

## Shift 15

*Music is cut off by a howl of dangerous laughter and singing from Man #1 as Hughie MacDonald, Amelia's birth father. He is very drunk, slipping from charm to belligerence in an instant.*

HUGHIE
*Singing.*
"I'se the b'y that builds the boat, and I'se the b'y that sails her! I'se the b'y that catches the fish and takes 'em home to Lizer."
*Abruptly he breaks off.*
Amelia, you little bitch! Why didn't you clean my boots? I told you what I'd do to you.
*He raises his arm to strike Amelia, who remains seated, remembering the moment. Raffaella — forty years younger — grabs him and struggles with him.*

RAFFAELLA
Don't you dare touch her, Hughie.

HUGHIE
I'm just puttin' my hand to her!

RAFFAELLA
You come in here stinking like a brewery . . .

HUGHIE
Goddam white nigger.

RAFFAELLA
You call me that again and I'll kill you!

HUGHIE
Wastin' my life on some goddam foreigner!

RAFFAELLA
Good enough to have your child.

HUGHIE
*If* it's mine. If you're not spreadin' your legs for somebody else.
*She hits him hard across the mouth.*
Fuckin' bitch. You hit me again and I'll lay you flat.

RAFFAELLA
*Screaming.*
Let us alone, or I swear I'll kill you.
*Raffaella attacks him, screaming and shouting, as they struggle again. He enjoys the fight, even laughing. He pushes her down against the kitchen table and throttles her, suddenly dangerous again. He turns to shout at Amelia.*

HUGHIE
Shall I kill her? You want me to kill her? Just tell me.

AMELIA
No! Please, Daddy, stop! Stop it!
*But Raffaella manages to pull away from him, grabbing a knife from the kitchen table. He stumbles to the floor. Suddenly she is on top of him, straddling him with knife raised.*

RAFFAELLA
You touch her again, and I swear to God I'll kill you. Understand me, you son of a bitch? I'll put this through your heart!

AMELIA
No! Mama, please! Don't hurt him!

## Shift 16

*Her cries are drowned out by a discord, then the opera music which fades down quickly.*

AMELIA
Why did you marry him at all?

RAFFAELLA
He had a good job in the Depression, which no one thought would ever end. And it was time for me to get out of the house.

AMELIA
I think you married Hughie to prove you were as "white" as anyone.

RAFFAELLA
Well, in my day, marrying a Scot was like a mixed race marriage.

AMELIA
Which is why his sisters and their kids called us "white niggers."

RAFFAELLA
*Pause then.*
Going back to school has done nothin' but give you a bad mouth. And too much imagination. You were only five or six years old back then.

AMELIA
They always said it behind your back, of course.

RAFFAELLA
Hand me the cinnamon.

AMELIA
I thought you used nutmeg.

RAFFAELLA
You never write it down.

AMELIA
I'm not the cook you are, Mama. It's a gift.

RAFFAELLA
It's practice and discipline, my girl.

AMELIA
Now you sound like your stepmother. Wasn't she a sour-faced bitch of a woman?

RAFFAELLA
The MacIssacs brought me up as best they could.

AMELIA
There — again!

RAFFAELLA
What?

AMELIA
"The MacIssacs" — like they were good neighbors. Never "Papa" or "Mama." Like you were just the little wop who did the house work.

RAFFAELLA
We don't use that kind of language.

AMELIA
But we do, Mama. All the Bortolatos talk like that — and the Covellos.

RAFFAELLA
We don't have to descend to their level.

AMELIA
Because we're the *inglese,* [English], and they're the wops!
You know the Bortolatos still call us *mangia-cakes?*

RAFFAELLA
All this digging around in the past isn't doing you any good.

AMELIA
I didn't come to fight about that anyway. Listen, I think it's
all over between me and Vinny.

*Shift 17*

VINNY
You walk out on me, and you walk out with nothing.

AMELIA
It's my right. Half of everything you own —

VINNY
*Cutting her off.*
Yeah? You better get some bright Jew-boy lawyer, because
your name is on nothing, except your fucking underwear.

AMELIA
If you want to drag us through court —

VINNY
You want my money? You go out and whore around for it.
You earn it like I did, with the sweat of my balls. I put the
roof over your head and the food in your fucking mouth!
Plus the trips to Italy. And all this goddam school shit. You
are costing me my balls, lady. And I mean both of them.

AMELIA
Sometimes I'd like to kill you.

VINNY
You are driving me crazy, lady.

AMELIA
Only thing that drives you is your dick!

VINNY
Hey!

AMELIA
I know who gets your dick going with that fat Polish mouth of hers!

VINNY
I am outta here.

AMELIA
Yeah, go on. Go on. Run back to your Polack bitch.

VINNY
At least she gives me some satisfaction.

AMELIA
I should have slit your throats — both of you.

VINNY
Go fuck yourself *twice*.

AMELIA
Son of a bitch! Son of a bitch!
*She tries to punch and slap him several times but he counters with one or two swift parries, then roughly shoves her away. He walks into Angelina's area where he transforms into Pietro. He puts a stranglehold on her. He is drunk and surly, but does not shout.*

## Shift 18

ANGELINA AND AMELIA
You're crazy. I could never do that.

PIETRO

Yes, you can. I see you talking with men, like some *puttana,* whore.

ANGELINA AND AMELIA

That's not true!

PIETRO

I know you're a whore already. So now you charge two, three dollars, maybe even five, if they stay a long time. You invite some men in here and get some money for me.

ANGELINA AND AMELIA

You're drunk again. Or crazy.

PIETRO

*Slapping her.*
*Zitta!* [Quiet.] Now you do your share. *Capisci?* You make any money yet?

ANGELINA AND AMELIA

You know I haven't.

PIETRO

You gonna get me the money for the rent? I tell you: if you do not do this, I will kill you. You understand? I hurt you so bad.

*He slaps her then he grabs her. He takes a knife from his pocket and slashes her face. Angelina screams and tries to protect herself. Amelia repeats the scream and gesture, reliving the moment with her. Their screams continue, until finally it is only Amelia who is screaming and flailing her arms madly, trying to defend herself from an attack. Toni runs in and realizes something is terribly wrong and pulls Amelia into a chair to calm her. She checks out the empty bottle of pills behind the computer and the bottle of grappa that is next to it. She curses to herself, then quickly walks Amelia out of the space.*

## *Shift 19*

*Woman #1, Elisabeth, walks briskly into the area with her attaché case and a bag of food. Briskly she starts to unpack these items as Toni re-enters. Through the dialogue Elisabeth sets out a dinner on paper plates of Chinese thick noodles and asparagus.*

TONI

It's like she went crazy. She's been drinking and taking pills.

ELISABETH

She's asking for help.

TONI

Every day. In every way. All right, all right, I love her. I'm just tired of her trying to be Miss Hi-Fi Italiano. Look.
*Pointing to various Italian items, like the commedia mask.*
No other wop on the block has all this stuff. They don't care about *commedia dell'arte* and Dante. Only culture they want is the CHIN picnic and two cars in the garage.

ELISABETH

Child, it is not a matter of love. It is about loyalty.

TONI

I don't want to become like her.

ELISABETH

Don't cut those roots, honey. One day you'll look in the mirror and see your mama.

TONI

All right! But it's not just the culture bullshit. She knows the marriage is all over but she's scared to leave. Even though this Don Sedgwick is crazy for her.

ELISABETH

You think they have been . . .
*Her expression indicates sleeping together.*

TONI
She won't tell me. But last weekend they saw each other
again.

ELISABETH
He would be a big improvement over Vinny.

TONI
Except if she dumps my father, she becomes *la divorziata*.

ELISABETH
No one in my neighborhood cared when I got a divorce. Just
another lady who dumped her man.

TONI
How about when Cheryl moved in?

ELISABETH
"There goes the neighborhood!"

TONI
So no one bothers you?

ELISABETH
Some people don't like the fact that she's white.

TONI
But lesbians are ok?

ELISABETH
When you don't have a penis, you're not a sexual threat.

TONI
But a *divorziata* is doubtful. What does it say about you? Or
your family?

AMELIA
*Entering with a tray of coffee cups.*
I don't want to talk about this.

TONI
*Mocking.*
Ma, being a *divorziata* doesn't make you a *puttana*. Just a "shady lady." Elisabeth, you want plates for that food?

ELISABETH
For all of us. And I'd love some fresh lemon for the asparagus.

TONI
I'll check the fridge.
*Leaving the room.*

ELISABETH
You want to talk about what's pushing you over the edge, sweetie?

AMELIA
Everything. The thesis. I keep getting stuck on this one case, and then Vinny . . . oh Jesus, I think it's all over but I'm afraid to walk out on him.

ELISABETH
Take my advice and dump him.

AMELIA
If I divorce Vinny, the family . . . it would really hurt them . . . and even the friends I grew up with . . .

ELISABETH
Not this one. And who is going to throw the first stone?

AMELIA
It's not like that! No one insults you in public. But you haven't lived up to your promise. You've failed the family and your friends somehow.

ELISABETH
Then move out of the neighborhood. Or at least sit down and eat.
*Toni re-enters with plates, cutlery, etc.*

AMELIA
All I need is some coffee.

ELISABETH
You'll need all the strength you can get. So *mangia!* [Eat!] It'll soak up the alcohol.

TONI
And the pills.

ELISABETH
*To Toni.*
*Basta!*
*To Amelia, as she starts to eat.*
Listen, I can work with you through the weekend. You've got lots of material you're not using yet. And I dug up several cases. Enough to compare how the courts handled Italian women versus Anglo women.

AMELIA
I'll have to start all over again!

ELISABETH
Nonsense. You just have to re-focus your material. Show how the justice system dealt with domestic crimes in the ethnic communities differently.

TONI
Another immigrant story.

ELISABETH
Not quite. Read the material. Italians are violent, dirty, immoral, and stupid, with no respect for law or decency. Ready to cut you up as soon as they look at you. Sound familiar?

TONI
Oh come on.

AMELIA
Elisabeth.

ELISABETH

I dug up some fascinating cases. Like this rich woman who killed her husband in Thunder Bay. Your mother was born there, wasn't she?

AMELIA

No, Sault Ste. Marie . . . I think. It's hard to pull family stories out of her. She doesn't like digging up the past.

## *Shift 20*

*Jump-cut: Raffaella starts to talk, drawing Amelia into her kitchen.*

RAFFAELLA

You're going to write about a murder?

AMELIA

It's more than that. It's about prejudice against Italians and abuse inside the community.
*Raffaella is stonily silent and continues working.*
Mama, it's not like I'm writing about Italian gangsters.

RAFFAELLA

Who were these people?

AMELIA

Their name was Napolitano. Angelina and Pietro. From a little village near Naples called Aversa. Ever hear of it?

RAFFAELLA

No. And what kind of job will this get you?
*Switching topics deliberately.*
Especially if you're on your own.

AMELIA

I have to get something from Vinny.

RAFFAELLA

Or whatever the lawyers leave you. If he was raising a hand to you —

AMELIA

There's more than one kind of abuse.

RAFFAELLA

He's always put a roof over your head and never spared a dollar for you or Toni.

AMELIA

I can't live in his house anymore!

RAFFAELLA

There's no room for you here.

AMELIA

You can bake for half the neighborhood and help anyone who comes crying to you.

RAFFAELLA

And come home to some quiet and privacy.

AMELIA

I feel like I'm going down the drain!

RAFFAELLA

If you're a good wife and mother, you don't worry about yourself. No one promised you a perfect marriage, my girl.

*Shift 21*

AMELIA

She is not impressed with me or my work. And Carole, my reader, hates my thesis so far. It's too ethnic. It's too literary.

ELISABETH

The Dragon Lady? Oh! I am tired of Anglo feminists who have their own agenda.

AMELIA

She says it would be different if I were writing about women of color.

ELISABETH

Women of color — Italian women two generations ago — same difference. Don't get me started. Just get me dessert.

TONI

I'll get the *gelato*.

AMELIA

It was easier writing about Italian literature.

ELISABETH

Yes. I loved your B.A. thesis about all those women. Clytemnestra especially.
    *Theatrically and with gestures.*
"Quick! Give me an axe! I will cut down Agamemnon and any who stand in my way!" Now there's a woman I can agree with.

TONI

    *From the kitchen.*
No wonder he had a girlfriend on the side.

AMELIA

    *Shouting at Toni.*
Shut up!
    *To Elisabeth.*
But I was writing about Alfieri. He did adaptations of Greek tragedy in Italian.

ELISABETH

Never heard of him.

AMELIA

Greatest playwright of the eighteenth century! And in Italian, we call her *Clitennestra*.

ELISABETH
*Relishing the name.*
*Clitennestra. Ah, sì!*

TONI
*Entering with gelato.*
Oh ma, what are you trying to prove?

AMELIA
I am proud of my heritage.

TONI
You are over the edge.

AMELIA
*Intensely quoting.*
*"Passatemi, presto, un'ascia assassina."* ["Quick! Give me an axe!"]

TONI
I don't do "wop-talk."

AMELIA
Never, never in this house do I want to hear that word.

TONI
Is *dago* politically correct?

AMELIA
Shut up, you.
*To Elisabeth. She leaves for the kitchen.*
You want an espresso?

ELISABETH
Bless you, yes.

TONI
Was she always this bad?

ELISABETH
*Enjoying the food.*
Mmmm. Always. Enthusiastic. Inquisitive. But with a kind
heart.

TONI
Read: "Stupid."

ELISABETH
Read: "Truly innocent." When we first met, I could tell she
was trying to see beyond the stereotype. It made me curious
about her. Plus, we were both minorities on that campus. Us
versus all those bright Jewish kids who were so confident!
Or maybe just loud.

TONI
The Bortolatos must have loved you when she brought you
home.

ELISABETH
I think she asked me to be her maid of honor just to piss them
off.

AMELIA
*Overhearing as she enters.*
I asked you because you were my best friend.

ELISABETH
Who they referred to as "La Melanzana . . . The Eggplant"
— behind my back, of course. So at the reception I kept
introducing myself: *"Mi chiamo Signorina Elisabetta Melanzana. Come stai?"* ["My name is Miss Elisabeth Eggplant. How
are you?"]

AMELIA
You were terrible.

ELISABETH
After three glasses of champagne, I didn't care.

*Enjoying the food.*
Mmmm. This will help me get through the night. And before
I forget, I have to call home.
*Juggling food and dialling simultaneously.*
Are you still seeing this Don?

AMELIA
Don Sedgwick. I don't think so.

TONI
*Singing sarcastically.*
"*Con te partirò.*" ["With you, I will go anywhere."]

AMELIA
*Eh tu, stai zitta!* [Hey you, be quiet.]

TONI
*Sì, signora Mussolini.*

ELISABETH
Hold on!
*Into the phone.*
Andrew, if you get home first from the game, cut the broccoli
and carrots up for steaming. The lamb chops are unfrozen,
so put them in the oven at 350 degrees — no higher! — for
thirty minutes at least. Cheryl will make the salad when she
gets home from work. If she's late, eat alone, and then you
can go out — until midnight. Love you, Baby. Hope you had
a good game. Bye!
*She blows a kiss in the phone and returns to her place. Amelia
looks up from the document she's been reading but she has
obviously been following Elisabeth's message with some admi-
ration, if not awe.*

AMELIA
My God, I wish I could be as firm as that in my house.

ELISABETH
We are a family, my dear, not a democracy. And my Andrew
counts as an endangered species. Now, let's get to work.

AMELIA
I still want to use the Napolitano case.

ELISABETH
As a reference point, fine. I brought lots of other cases. The
number of women who killed their husbands . . . amazing!

AMELIA
But the evidence is sketchy or just downright contradictory.

ELISABETH
Give me an example.

## *Shift 22*

PROSECUTOR MEREDITH
Constable White, you saw the deceased lying on the bed. Did
you see any injuries?

CONSTABLE WHITE
Oh yes, Sir. Five or six cuts, all down the side of the face.

PROSECUTOR MEREDITH
Five or six cuts?

CONSTABLE WHITE
Yes, Sir.

MEREDITH
The coroner says there were more than seven. Many more.

CONSTABLE WHITE
Hard to tell, Sir. His skull was pretty well crushed in.

MEREDITH
As if someone had bludgeoned him? Repeatedly? Mercilessly?

CONSTABLE WHITE
Well . . . uh . . . yes, Sir.

MEREDITH
Were there wounds on other parts of his body?

CONSTABLE WHITE
Yes, Sir.

MEREDITH
Did they appear to be fresh?

WHITE
The blood was dried on them, Sir.

MEREDITH
Was there much blood on his clothing?

WHITE
Quite a bit. It had run down the pillow.

MEREDITH
*Showing it.*
Is this the axe that was in the bedroom?

WHITE
Yes, Sir. That is the axe.

MEREDITH
We can all see that it is covered with blood. But was that the condition it was in?

WHITE
Yes, Sir.

MEREDITH
What are these things here?

WHITE

That's some of the clothes she had on when I arrested her.
They were all splashed with blood too.

## Shift 23

*A shimmer of cymbals as lights come up on Angelina as
Clytemnestra, who has wrapped the cape around her. As she
recites and gestures theatrically in Italian, Amelia echoes her
in English.*

CLYTEMNESTRA

*Passatemi, presto, un'ascia assassina.
È da veder se stronchiamo o finiamo stroncati.
A questo passo di dolore mi sono spinta ormai!*

AMELIA

*Overlapping.*

Quick! Give me an axe!
I will cut down Agamemnon and any who stand in my way!
We'll see who is to be the butcher and who the slaughtered.
O Gods, to what depths have you plunged me!

## Shift 24

AMELIA

*Solo.*

When you think about it . . . it's hard to kill someone. She
doesn't have a gun . . . too expensive. When you're poor, you
have to use whatever's at hand. A knife. But if you've never
done it before, how do you know where to push the knife?
Might run into bone. Or just spill a lot of blood. Then he can
attack *you*. Especially someone bigger like Pietro. And what
if the knife breaks? What do you have left? Yes! The axe in
the woodpile. Sshhh! Careful not to wake him up, Angelina.
Creep up slowly, raise the axe, aim for his head and then. . .

## Shift 25

*Distorted sound of gavel banging. Lights come up. Angelina is in the witness chair.*

MCFADDEN
Mrs. Napolitano, what was the relationship between you and your husband from the time you were married until you moved to Sault Ste. Marie?

ANGELINA
He was a pretty good man before. After I was marry, he was a good man. But we had a few quarrels and words and talking sometimes.

MCFADDEN
Did he ever strike you?

ANGELINA
No.

MCFADDEN
Did you ever strike *him?*

ANGELINA
*Pause.*
No.

MCFADDEN
When did you first have trouble with your husband?

ANGELINA
After we come to Sault Ste. Marie two year ago. He see lots of other people having houses and the money. He wants to make moneys out of me, and I was a bad women, he say. He say he is always poor and working hard every day. And he want to make some store, you know.

JUSTICE BRITTON
I beg your pardon.

MCFADDEN
Your Honor, I think she means to open a small business, like a grocery store. Is that right, Mrs. Napolitano?

ANGELINA
*Sì.* Yes.

JUSTICE BRITTON
But, Mr. McFadden, this is no evidence in defense.

MCFADDEN
It is evidence of some provocation, your Honor.

JUSTICE BRITTON
No.

MAN#2
There was a man asleep in bed and she took an axe to him.

WOMAN#2
When she could have called on the protection of the law.

MAN#2
They were living happily together as husband and wife.

WOMAN #2
So what motive for murder could there be?

MAN #2
If anybody injured six months ago . . .

WOMAN#2
. . . Could give that as an excuse for slaying a person . . .

JUSTICE BRITTON
. . . It would be anarchy complete!

MCFADDEN
Very well, your Honor.
*Back to Angelina.*
This was about a year ago when he started to talk this way?

ANGELINA
Yes.

MCFADDEN
What happened about October of last year?

ANGELINA
In October he was crazy. He say, "if I leave you, what are you going to do?" He say that I am a *puttana*, that —

JUSTICE BRITTON
I beg your pardon?

MCFADDEN
I believe that it is the Italian word for a woman of the streets.

JUSTICE BRITTON
I see. Continue.

MCFADDEN
*Prompting Angelina.*
So your husband said that ...

ANGELINA
. . . That I am a bad woman. I say, "No, no, I am not!"

## Shift 26

*Man #1 as Pietro has walked up behind her and grabs her again, pulling her up and off her feet. He is grimly drunk. They are in the middle of a fight again.*

PIETRO
Yes, you are a bad woman. Maybe you should get another man. Now, I leave you for a while. I give you ten dollars. You start your business with men. When I come back, maybe you will have more. Or I will kill you. Listen! You ask for two or three dollars, or even five, if they stay for the night.

### ANGELINA
I cannot do this.

### PIETRO
Yes, you can. Because it is a good thing for us. All of us. If we cannot pay the rent, then we will all live on the street. If I come back and you have done nothing, I will kill you. Remember: I marry you so I own you.

*With an abrupt move, he drops her so she sits in the witness chair as lights change.*

## Shift 27

### AMELIA
I still don't understand why she couldn't plead self-defense.

### ELISABETH
"Spousal abuse" wasn't accepted as a basis for defense.

### AMELIA
But Pietro threatened to kill her again and again.

### ELISABETH
Did he come at her with a knife? I mean, in the last minutes before she killed him? The theory of self-defense — of that time — applied only when the danger was immediate, not five months previous.

### TONI
*As she looks through the material.*
Where's the rest of the trial stuff?

### AMELIA
It only took two days. One morning actually. First day Angelina had no lawyer. So the judge appoints one and they start the next day.

TONI
One fucking day to prepare a murder defense! That must be illegal.

ELISABETH
Sweetie, this is not *Law and Order*. It's not even Ally McBeal. We were still under British law, so your lawyer, that is, barrister might not even see you until the morning of the trial.

AMELIA
They couldn't even figure out the number of times she axed him.

TONI
Why didn't her lawyer catch any of this?

ELISABETH
Not enough time. Not enough experience. And not much evidence on his side. Also, you mustn't look too radical in defending a minority person. Uh-uh, honey! Get you a bad reputation!

TONI
But the women on the jury —

ELISABETH
Child, will you get some history in your head! It's a time when the Supreme Court is telling women they are not legal persons. You could vote but not run for office. And most provinces didn't allow women on juries until after the Second World War.

TONI
All right! Then Angelina's got nothing going for her.

ELISABETH
Bingo! If you don't have the language, if you don't have the money, if you don't have the education, if you do not run the system, the system will not work for you.

TONI
She should have cut his balls off. Wham!

## Shift 28

*Sharp sound of axe-cracking. Man #2 as Prosecutor Meredith is in the midst of his cross examination. He holds an axe behind him.*

PROSECUTOR MEREDITH
You had quarreled all through the morning? For several hours?

ANGELINA
Four . . . maybe five hours.

MEREDITH
He threatened to kill you?

ANGELINA
And the child inside me!

MEREDITH
This is the axe you used to murder your husband?

ANGELINA
That is the axe.

MEREDITH
*Building slowly.*
So you crept quietly upstairs. As quietly as you could. You went up to the bed. How close to the bed? As close as I am to you?

ANGELINA

Yes.

MEREDITH

And you struck him in the head with the axe?

ANGELINA

Yes.

MEREDITH

And you struck him seven times — at least?

ANGELINA

I no sure.

MEREDITH

The doctor says there were seven wounds. And even more!
Will you say you did not strike him seven times — at least?
In a state of rage and vengeful anger!

ANGELINA

I no count. I . . .

MEREDITH

*Shouting.*

Seven — at least! And many more perhaps! The work of a
demented murderess overflowing with hate and rage!

ANGELINA

*Overlapping him.*

*No lo so. No lo so. Lasciami. Lasciami.* [I don't know. Let me
alone.]

> *As he strides away, she explodes in tears. But her voice is
> drowned out by . . .*

## *Shift 29*

*Operatic music — Act 2 of Puccini's* Tosca *— from Raffaella's radio crossfades over the previous sound. She works vigorously at her kitchen table.*

AMELIA
She just wants to say hello and hand over some pictures and documents.

RAFFAELLA
I'm too busy to see her.

AMELIA
Effie is your own sister —

RAFFAELLA
Half-sister.

AMELIA
And why does she call you "Jenny"?

RAFFAELLA
That's what the MacIssacs named me. I don't know why she has to come poking around in other people's business.

AMELIA
She hasn't seen you for forty years! She's only in town for the weekend for her son's wedding. If she's thoughtful enough to bring you some old family records and —

RAFFAELLA
I am trying to get Easter dinner for thirty people! Just tell her I'm bad off with my arthritis and can't see anyone.

AMELIA
Have it your way.
*Pause as she decides.*
And, Mama, I have to tell you: I'm thinking of consulting a lawyer about me and Vinny.

RAFFAELLA
If you want to ruin a perfectly good life, you go ahead.

AMELIA
I am not a whore because I want to get rid of a bad husband.

RAFFAELLA
Go ahead and ruin all we worked to build up. I don't want to know about it.

AMELIA
Can't you give me a little support when I need it?

RAFFAELLA
You won't take any advice from me.

AMELIA
I just want some attention. Stop making cookies for everybody and look at me. Jesus Christ, how can you hear me over that goddam racket!

RAFFAELLA
I thought you liked Italian music.
> *Her sarcasm does the job. Amelia leaves her. Raffaella continues working for a moment, but her body suddenly stiffens, then twitches as the music of Tosca crescendoes behind her. Knife in one hand, her arms fly up, poised to strike someone, and then she brings them down with a crashing blow on the table.*

## Shift 30

AMELIA
> *Back to Elisabeth.*
Why doesn't she want to see Effie?

ELISABETH
Too much emotional baggage maybe.

**AMELIA**

But Mama always says how kind they were to her.

**EFFIE**

What a lovely house!

*Woman #2 has entered as Effie, a distracted but happy chatter-box, a few years older than Raffaella.*

**AMELIA**

*Still to Elisabeth, describing Effie.*

So Effie shows up on my doorstep two days ago . . .

**EFFIE**

And you have a garden too.

**AMELIA**

*To Elisabeth.*

A very sweet lady.

*To Effie.*

Would you like some biscotti and espresso?

**EFFIE**

Well, maybe I could try that.

**AMELIA**

I have some real grappa from our last trip to Italy. Shall I put a wee drop in?

*Effie is puzzled by the word grappa.*

It's like Newfie "screech." But mellower.

**EFFIE**

Let's give her a try there!

*Business of Amelia bringing food and serving it; they sample the grappa and other goodies as they talk. Amelia turns to Elisabeth to narrate the scene.*

**AMELIA**

So we get caught up on all the family history and gossip. All the while she's making an inventory of the furniture in the room. Obviously not what she expected from Raffaella's little girl.

EFFIE
These mirrors and pictures — like out of a museum . . .

AMELIA
*Back to Effie.*
From our first trip to Italy. Everything's from little shops in Florence.

EFFIE
Aren't you lucky. Your husband must be doing real well.

AMELIA
He sells cars and he owns the business.

EFFIE
And you were doin' some courses last year.

AMELIA
I finished my B.A. in Italian Lit.

EFFIE
Isn't that lovely, dear. So now you can teach.

AMELIA
I'm doing a Master's in Women's Studies. At OISE.

EFFIE
Oh, so you can teach that. Or do social work?

AMELIA
If I get my thesis done.

EFFIE
Won't that be lovely!
*This reminds Effie of her reason for being here. She takes a large, worn manila envelope out of her handbag and hands it to Amelia.*

Before I forget. Here's the papers I found when I was cleaning out the attic. It's mostly photos and school certificates.

AMELIA
This looks like her high school graduation.

EFFIE
I helped mother make her dress.

AMELIA
But she's listed as "J. MacIssac."

EFFIE
That's right. "J" for Jennifer. "Jinny-Jenny" I used to call her.

AMELIA
Then how did she become Raffaella?
*Holding a worn business-size envelope up.*
Why is this sealed?

EFFIE
It was just there with the other things. Anyway, her brother
came to see her. And suddenly she wanted to change her
name.
*This stuns Amelia so hard, she can find nothing to say for a
moment. She looks at Elisabeth, then tries to refocus on the
scene with Effie.*

AMELIA
But Mama always told me she was an only child.

## *Shift 31*

RAFFAELLA
The trick is to always keep a little flour on your rolling pin.
So your dough is nice and thin. Then you roll it one way . . .
then the opposite direction.

AMELIA
*As a child of ten.*
These are gonna be great cannoles. Did Mother MacIssac teach you?

RAFFAELLA
*Laughing.*
No! Our neighbor next door.

AMELIA
The lady you named me after?

RAFFAELLA
Keep rolling it nice and even now.

AMELIA
Did she ever see me?

RAFFAELLA
No. I got married long after the Roccos had moved away.

AMELIA
I thought their name was Rocastella.

RAFFAELLA
*Pause.*
No, Rocco. Luigi and Amelia Rocco. Now, let's finish mixing the ricotta.

AMELIA
With the three handsome sons.
*Teasing.*
Except none of them fell in love with you!

RAFFAELLA
Not Italian enough, I guess. I need the chocolate now.

AMELIA
So you had to marry Hughie MacDonald. Then you had me!

RAFFAELLA

That's enough story-telling for now. Where's the chocolate chips?

AMELIA

He drank a lot and hollered a lot, I remember. And he hit you. Papa is a lot nicer. Except he smells like garlic.

RAFFAELLA

You're lucky to have Giuseppe Bortolato as a step-father, believe you me. He gave you a name and a roof over your head. Now where's the chocolate?

AMELIA
*Handing her a small paper bag.*
Here.

RAFFAELLA

This isn't half of what we had. What did you do with it?
*No answer from Amelia.*
Did you eat it? Answer me, young lady.

AMELIA

I just took a few for me and my friend Dorothy, and then she grabbed the bag. . .

RAFFAELLA

So you stole it! And now you're trying to lie to me. A liar and a thief, is that what you've become?

AMELIA
*Tearfully.*
No, Mama, I just . . .

RAFFAELLA
*Anger building.*
You're disgracing the whole family. You have to keep up *la bella figura* [a good face to the world.] If you don't have a

good reputation, you have nothing in this world. That's the one thing I've tried to teach you.

### AMELIA
Mama, please, I only wanted —

### RAFFAELLA
*In a rage.*
I'm ashamed of you. You hear me? Ashamed! I don't even want to look at you. Up to your room. When your father gets home, he'll take care of you good. Get out of here before you get the back of my hand. Out before I whip the bejesus out of you!
*She raises her hand to strike the child. Amelia cringes, the memory too immediate, as lights crossfade back to the present.*

## Shift 32

### EFFIE
Oh yes, she was the good girl in our family. And at school and church. Which didn't make her popular.

### AMELIA
Why did Mama tell me she was an only child?

### EFFIE
That's what we thought too. Until this man comes to the door, asking for her. He says his name is, oh dear, something like Michael.

### AMELIA
Michele?

### EFFIE
Could be. They go upstairs for a long talk. When they came down, Jenny's eyes were all swollen. And the man says he's on his way to the West Coast so he can't stay for dinner. A

few days later your mother announces that she's chosen a
new name.

AMELIA
Raffaella.

EFFIE
And could I have a little more of that delicious, uh . . .

AMELIA
With a wee drop of grappa.
    *She pours coffee and adds grappa.*

EFFIE
Our parents didn't argue with her. They realized, I guess, she
wanted to — what's the expression these days? — to find her
identity or her ethnic roots, whatever. So we all humored her.
She could be a strange girl sometimes.

AMELIA
Did she have any Italian friends?

EFFIE
There was that lovely Eye-talian family next door to us. The
mother taught Jenny a lot about cooking. They would even
talk some Eye-talian.

AMELIA
Mama named me after her.

EFFIE
Oh no, dear. Her name was Lucy. I mean, Lucia. Like the song
we learned in school from the good sisters.
    *Singing.*
"Santa Lucia, Santa Lucia . . ."

AMELIA
Maybe she had a daughter or there was some other girl.

EFFIE
Oh no. Only boys. Dark, almost swarthy, but good-looking in their own way. And Mr. Petrone, of course, who made wonderful wine and would give us some twice a year.
*This is another shock for Amelia who takes a deep breath. She knows she has to verify this, so she asks very deliberately.*

AMELIA
What was their name?

EFFIE
*Enunciating carefully.*
Petrone.

AMELIA
No, no. It was Rocco. Or maybe Roccostella. Petrone was Mama's name from her birth family.

EFFIE
Well, then, it was the neighbors' name too. We heard it every day.

AMELIA
But Mama's birth family . . .

EFFIE
She'd been with several foster families before us — so I wouldn't know about that.

AMELIA
What about her birth certificate?

EFFIE
Might be in that envelope, dear.
*Savoring the taste.*
Oh my, this coffee is good.

## Shift 33

*As Effie leaves the area, Amelia hands Elisabeth the envelope to open.*

TONI
You've had that envelope two days and you haven't opened it!

AMELIA
Somehow, I'm afraid of what's in it.

TONI
Give it to me.

ELISABETH
That's not your business, Child.

TONI
Then it's none of your business either.

AMELIA
Stop that. How dare you?

ELISABETH
No. She's right. It isn't my business. Not at this moment anyway. I'm the expert on legal matters. Not family history. I should be getting home.

AMELIA
You can't walk out on me.

ELISABETH
I'm not deserting the ship. But it's getting late, and I will be back tomorrow if you need me.

AMELIA
I need you right now.

ELISABETH

No, no. I think you need to clear up family matters first. Go through that material from Effie. Then talk to your mother I would think.

AMELIA

You're angry with me.

ELISABETH

No, Sweetie, I am tired and I've done what I can do for the moment. I've got tomorrow off, so I'll be back. I'll let myself out. You two just worry about family business first.

AMELIA
*Kissing her.*
Good night. Thank you so much.

ELISABETH
*Embracing her.*
You call me in the morning.

TONI

Elisabeth, I'm sorry.

ELISABETH

No need. But you stay here and help your mother.

TONI

Yes, Ma'am.
*Elisabeth exits with her coat and attaché case. A pause as Toni opens the envelope while Amelia looks on expectantly. Toni takes out some items.*

TONI

It's a report card from some school in New York.

AMELIA

Mama never told me she lived in the States.

TONI

Oh yeah, and she lied about her age to get a job when you first came to Toronto. Made it easier to marry Grandpa Bortolato.

AMELIA

Why didn't you tell me this before?

TONI

I was thirteen, and it was fun having a secret! Anyway, you weren't into this family ethnic crap then.

AMELIA

Nothing fits together!
*Looking at another document.*
Oh Jesus, Mary! Now I am gonna go crazy.

TONI

What?

AMELIA

Look at this.

TONI

Looks like Grandma's birth certificate.

AMELIA

Look at the family name.
*She hands Toni a birth certificate. She reads the certificate quickly, and then again in disbelief.*

## Shift 34

LAWYER MCFADDEN

Mrs. Napolitano, how many children have you?

ANGELINA

Four. And the one I am expecting.

MCFADDEN
What are their ages?

ANGELINA
There is the baby, Domenico. Nearly one year old. Michele has five years. Amelia has eight year. And then my oldest, Raffaella.

## Shift 35

*Lights up on Raffaella, who turns to look at Amelia, who is staring at her in astonishment.*

AMELIA
Mama?

Blackout

# Act Two

## Shift 36

*On the soundtrack, a shimmer of cymbals. Pinspot on Angelina who sits in her chair and quietly finishes her testimony to us.*

ANGELINA

So I took the axe, I am going upstairs. And I think, "If he wake up, he will see me with the axe in my hand and kill me, and if he kill me, my baby, inside of me, die too." And because I could not stand the trouble any longer, I just went upstairs and I hit him with the axe.

## Shift 37

FRANCINE THOMPSON

"Raffaella Napolitano, age ten, is hereby committed by the Children's Aid Society to the care and custody of Angus and Theresa MacIssac of North Bay at 317 Johnson St. We recommend that contact with her sister and brothers be discouraged. However, each child is to be permitted a written correspondence with Angelina Napolitano since her sentence has been commuted. However, personal visits cannot be encouraged."

## Shift 38

RAFFAELLA
*Walking angrily into the room.*
That belongs to me.

**AMELIA**
It belongs to me too.

**RAFFAELLA**
Why do you have to poke your nose into everything?

**AMELIA**
Because you can't tell the truth about anything. Sit down, Mama . We have to talk now.
*As Amelia stares at her mother, her look of puzzlement is slowly transformed into an hysterical giggle that takes her over.*

**RAFFAELLA**
Are you going crazy?

**AMELIA**
It's just so ridiculous. Murders and axes and headlines.

**TONI**
Too weird.

**RAFFAELLA**
It's not funny.

**AMELIA**
What am I supposed to say? It's like someone kicking you in the stomach.

**RAFFAELLA**
Exaggerating again.

**AMELIA**
Mama! I don't want it to be true. I wish I hadn't started all this.
*A gesture toward computer desk.*
But there we are. Let's finish the story.
*Raffaella stares at her, refusing to say a word more.*
Anyway, I have to admit, I'm dying of curiosity.

RAFFAELLA
Like a child.

TONI
Me too, Grandma, it's only natural. Come on.

AMELIA
Why couldn't you tell me the truth?

RAFFAELLA
I thought I was saving an innocent child from disgrace and shame.

AMELIA
*Pulling material from her research file.*
Your faces were in the newspaper again and again. This is you, yes? And the two little boys and your sister . . .

RAFFAELLA
Amelia. I named you after her.

AMELIA
How did you think you could hide all this?

RAFFAELLA
I did it pretty well for fifty years.

AMELIA
Secrets and lies!

RAFFAELLA
I didn't start it. The Children's Aid Society changed our names and put us in different homes all over the province. I tried to keep in contact with Amelia. But her step-parents kept moving.

TONI
You lost your sister? The CAS should have kept records —

RAFFAELLA

Little girl, files get mislaid or burned. People forget or retire. Then Mama was pardoned after — how many years was it? — eleven or twelve? By that time we had all grown up and lost touch with each other.

TONI

Grandma, why did they separate you like that?

RAFFAELLA

Times were different then. Adultery — murder — they disgraced the whole family, not just the wrongdoer. And that disgrace would continue for generations. Unless you could start a new life with a new name. There's no reason to dig up the past.

AMELIA

Yes, for your own good, Mama. Mine too, maybe.
    *Approaching her.*
You had to carry this all alone for so long.

RAFFAELLA

Don't touch me. You don't understand anything.

AMELIA

Because everything was hidden from me. I can't help you if . . .

RAFFAELLA

Don't need your help.

AMELIA

*"Bisogna fare la bella figura."* That's the only Italian you ever taught me: "You have to maintain a good face to the world." Even if it's all lies.

TONI

What's the big deal? Your grandmother killed an abusive son-of-a-bitch who deserved it. She should have cut his dick off first.

AMELIA

Shut up.

TONI

As usual, I get treated like a piece of shit.

AMELIA

Stop that, for chrissakes!

RAFFAELLA

What about my privacy?

AMELIA

*Showing the carton of material.*

Look, Mama. The whole world knew about Angelina Napolitano. Come on. Enough secrets and lies.

RAFFAELLA

You'll believe everybody else before you believe me. Anyway, you have no idea how bad things were. No money, too many kids, and him, drunk or acting crazy, babbling away.

## Shift 39

*Lights have crossfaded up on Man #1 as Pietro who is talking to Raffaella as a child. She listens for a moment, then walks away to join her mother at the kitchen table. He tries to get her attention. Angelina puts on a pair of glasses and sits down to read a book aloud with Raffaella.*

PIETRO

I was crazy for her, Raffaella. *Stupefatto! Come se dice?* [Stunned. How do you say it?] Bang! *Un colpo di fulmine.* [A thunderbolt]. Like you struck by lightning. When she makes

the walk in the town square . . . with her mother . . . I bow
. . . tip my hat: *"Buona sera, Signorina Valetti . . . Signora Valetti
. . . fa bel tempo stasera."*

ANGELINA
*Overlapping him.*
"A View of the Colosseum by Orville Dewey. The day after I
arrived in Rome, I went to see the Colosseum by moonlight.
It is the monarch —"
*To Raffaella.*
*Che cose è "monarch"?* [What is a "monarch"?]

RAFFAELLA
*As a child.*
A monarch is a king, I think.

PIETRO
But after we marry, she talk too free with everyone. The
butcher, the vegetable man. Laughing and pulling at her
dress, like a *puttana* in the street. She speak English so I no
understand her. Even with my own children.

RAFFAELLA
Did you ever go to Rome, Mama?

ANGELINA
Naples many times, but Rome too far.

PIETRO
And reading, always reading books in fucking English.

ANGELINA
*Continuing to read.*
"It is the monarch, the majesty of all ruins. There is nothing
like it."
*Pietro comes forward to rip the book out of her hands.*

PIETRO
*Perché parli inglese sempre? E che fai con questi libri?* [Why do you always speak English? And what are you doing with these books?]

ANGELINA
*Per aiutare gli bambini.* [To help the children.]

RAFFAELLA
*As a child.*
Teacher says we should always talk English, especially at home.

PIETRO
*Slapping her.*
*Zitta!* [Shut up!]

ANGELINA
Stop hitting her!

PIETRO
*Italiano! Parla Italiano! Sempre!* [Italian. Speak Italian. Always!]

ANGELINA
*Basta, cretino! Bruta bestia!* [Enough, idiot. Stupid animal.]

PIETRO
*Vaffanculo.* [Go fuck yourself.]
*As he hits her, she becomes enraged. Suddenly they are beating each other, with their fists or anything that comes to hand. They continue shouting curses at each other. Raffaella looks at them, terrified even in her memory.*

RAFFAELLA
No. Mama! Please, don't! Stop it. Both of you. Stop it!

## *Shift 40*

*Man #1 transforms into Hughie Macdonald. Again, we are in Raffaella's kitchen in North Bay, in the 1940s. He is singing in a happily drunk condition until he suddenly reverses into a rage.*

### HUGHIE
Singing.
"I don't want your maggoty fish, that's not good for winter;
I could buy as good as that down in Bonavista."
*Shouting.*
Amelia, you little bitch! I told you to clean my boots or I'll . . .

### RAFFAELLA
Don't you dare touch her, Hughie.

### HUGHIE
I'm just puttin' my hand to her!

### RAFFAELLA
Don't you get near her!

### HUGHIE
She's my child. I'll do as I like with her.
*She hits him hard across the mouth.*
Fuckin' bitch. You hit me again and I'll lay you flat.

### RAFFAELLA
*Screaming.*
Let us alone, or I swear I'll kill you.
*Raffaella attacks him, screaming and shouting as they struggle again. He pushes her down against the kitchen table and throttles her.*

### HUGHIE
Shall I kill her, Amelia? You want me to kill her? Just tell me.

### AMELIA
No! Please, Daddy, stop! Stop it!

*Raffaella manages to pull away from him, grabbing a knife from the kitchen table. He stumbles to the floor. Suddenly she is on top of him, straddling him with knife raised.*

RAFFAELLA

You touch her again, and I swear to God I'll kill you. Understand me, you son of a bitch? I'll put this knife through your heart!

AMELIA

No! Mama, please! Don't hurt him!

## *Shift 41*

*A sharp rapping of the gavel reverberates. Lights crossfade to Elisabeth. The defense lawyer questions Angelina.*

MCFADDEN

Mrs. Napolitano, your husband attacked you some five months before his death, in November of the previous year. Please describe what he did to you on that occasion.

ANGELINA

He start to fight me. He cut me all over. He make cut on my face.

MCFADDEN

Which you will carry for the rest of your life.
*Angelina nods. Pause.*
Did you strike back at him?

ANGELINA

*After a long pause.*
No.

MCFADDEN

Where were you when he attacked you?

ANGELINA
In our house.

MCFADDEN
After he stabbed you, where did you go?

ANGELINA
In hospital.

MCFADDEN
But where were you found before that?

ANGELINA
I go to run away.

MCFADDEN
You made a complaint against your husband?

ANGELINA
Yes.

MCFADDEN
Mrs. Napolitano, you were pregnant at the time of this attack last November, were you not?

ANGELINA
Yes, Sir. Two months in the family way.

MCFADDEN
But your husband was released on suspended sentence, wasn't he?
    *Angelina nods, then McFadden looks deliberately at jury.*
So he did not spend one day in jail after scarring your face for life! And trying to make you a prostitute. Mrs. Napolitano, we can see that you are close to the end of your term. When is your baby due?

ANGELINA
Six, maybe eight weeks, Sir.

## Shift 42

AMELIA
Wait, Mama. I've read everything available about this case. What I've never been able to understand is how could any Italian man — especially back then — ask his wife to prostitute herself. The last thing a poor man had was his honor. *Bisogna fare la bella figura.* Remember?

TONI
Bullshit. He was a crazy pimp who used his wife like a dog.

RAFFAELLA
No. Something was wrong with him, I think. He couldn't hang onto a job, fighting with landlords and neighbors, over ten years of moving, from the States to Canada, and with nothing to show for it.

AMELIA
You never told me you were born in New York.

RAFFAELLA
I didn't think I'd have to lie so much. Should have planned it better.

AMELIA
Wouldn't it have been easier to tell me the truth?

RAFFAELLA
What good is the truth? Especially for a child.

AMELIA
But the least you owe me now —

RAFFAELLA
*Cutting her off.*
I owed you a decent bringing up. Which you got. When did you lack for food or a clean house or a . . .

AMELIA
. . . Or a lot of anxiety and self-doubt and —

RAFFAELLA
*Losing control.*
I'm going crazy with all these questions. You think it's any pleasure for me to remember all that. Leave me alone. I made a good life for you here, knock wood: everybody healthy and enough money in the bank.

AMELIA
While you look down at me — as if I can never do enough. Jesus! Even when I was a kid, what did I have to do to get a hug from you? Much less a kiss. As if I had done something to be ashamed of.

RAFFAELLA
I wasn't the one who got pregnant halfway through university.

AMELIA
Exactly. When I was panicky about marrying Vinny, I came to you —

RAFFAELLA
When it was too late. And God knows, it didn't start there. You drove me crazy when you were a teenager. Running around like a tramp.

AMELIA
What do you call an Italian girl who stays out till midnight? *A puttana!*

RAFFAELLA
We tried to bring you up decently.

AMELIA
You tried to raise me like a nun! Even in if I came in late from a date.

*A sharp discord on the soundtrack. Raffaella walks into the pool of light, an anxious mother from twenty-five years ago.*

## Shift 43

RAFFAELLA
Where have you been, young lady? Two hours late! We thought something terrible happened to you.

AMELIA
Ma, we went for ice cream after the show, then we —

RAFFAELLA
Your father and me are going crazy with worry, and you're running around like a tramp.

AMELIA
Ma, nothing happened.

RAFFAELLA
You think I don't know what goes on out there?

AMELIA
We were just driving along College Street in Louie's car and having fun.

RAFFAELLA
I can't trust you outside this house. Lying and sneaking around —

AMELIA
That's not true.

RAFFAELLA
Ruining this family's reputation. No one wants to marry a tramp.

AMELIA
For chrissakes, Ma, we just had a little fun.

RAFFAELLA
Don't swear at me. What kind of girl comes home after midnight?

AMELIA
Other girls get to stay out late.

RAFFAELLA
A *puttana* who doesn't care about the honor of her family, that's who. A whore! Never thinking about us, how we would be disgraced.
*Slapping her.*
Goddamit, I work my fingers to the bone for you. Move to Toronto, just for you. I marry Bortolato so you can have a good home and security and —

AMELIA
All right, Mama. That's enough.

## Shift 44

*Back in the present, Amelia is shaking her mother to calm her down. But Raffaella is somewhere between rage and pain in a world of her own.*

RAFFAELLA
What do I get for it? Lies and you playing the tramp on College Street. Disgracing our name.

TONI
Come on, Grandma. It's all over. Who cares what happened back then?

RAFFAELLA
I have to be Jesus on a silver platter for all of you. Carrying you. Being responsible for you . . .

AMELIA
Mama, stop it please. I don't know you like this.

RAFFAELLA
Why do you think you know anything about me?

AMELIA
I'm not accusing you of anything wrong.

RAFFAELLA
So now you don't think anything is my fault.

TONI
Grandma, all we want to know is the real story.

AMELIA
What's upsetting me, Mama, is that you lied to me, withheld the truth deliberately.

RAFFAELLA
Oh, if it's the truth you want, you stupid little girl, it's simple enough.

## Shift 45

*Angelina brings in a white communion veil which she places on Raffaella's head.*

ANGELINA
*Ma guarda, com'è bella!* [Look how lovely it is!] Your First Communion is such an important day. It means you are a young lady, almost a woman.

RAFFAELLA
Except I wish we didn't have to make our first confession to that Father Finegan. His breath stinks!

ANGELINA
*Grim humor.*
Like the priest in my village.

RAFFAELLA

And Sister Gertrude Marie says our parents should go to confession and communion, too. Especially if they're in a state of mortal sin because they don't go to mass on Sunday.

ANGELINA

Your father is tired from working all week.

RAFFAELLA

I hate him anyway.

ANGELINA

Sometimes you treat him bad. No respect.

RAFFAELLA

He acts so crazy sometimes.

ANGELINA

The drink make him act that way.

RAFFAELLA

No, not when he's drunk. Sometimes at night, he comes into my room . . .

> *Abruptly Pietro — as in a nightmare moment — comes up behind Raffaella and traps her in a neck lock.*

PIETRO

Why you treat me so bad, Raffaella? Your poor papa — he work so hard for you. All day, all night sometime. Come home so tired. And you, you not even give me a little kiss, a little hug. Mama too busy with the *bambini*. I need my little *principessa* so bad, *un piccolo bacio*.

ANGELINA

*Silenzio! Cativa!* [Quiet! Bad girl.]

RAFFAELLA

I hate him. He won't leave me alone.

ANGELINA
*Bugiarda!* [Liar.]

RAFFAELLA
I'm not lying.

ANGELINA
If you lie like this, you disgrace us forever. Bring dishonor on us.

RAFFAELLA
But it's true.
*Before she can finish, Angelina has slapped her, then turns away from her, muttering to herself.*

ANGELINA
*Vergogna, infamia.* [Shame, disgrace.] Is not possible, you hear me? You make stories like that, and you are worse than a whore in the streets.
*She walks away, leaving a bewildered Raffaella. Man#2 as Father Finegan sits in Angelina's chair.*

## *Shift 46*

ANGELINA
*Making the sign of the cross.*
Bless me, Father, for I have sinned.

FATHER FINEGAN
How long since your last confession?

ANGELINA
Many years. When we first come to America. I am sorry. My English not so good.

FR. FINEGAN
That's all right. So you haven't been to mass regularly?

ANGELINA
No. I have four children.

FR. FINEGAN
All the more reason to set them a good example. Do you
understand that? "Good example."

ANGELINA
*Sì, sì.* I know.

FR. FINEGAN
Anything else of importance?

ANGELINA
With my husband. He get mad and drunk. He hit me. Then
I hit him back. Sometimes, even my children, when I get so
tired or —

FR. FINEGAN
Yes, yes, I understand. But your husband — is he a good
provider?

ANGELINA
He . . . a good worker, but not so much now.

FR. FINEGAN
These are trials to test us that God sends.

ANGELINA
He want me to be a bad woman.

FR. FINEGAN
I don't understand.

ANGELINA
My husband, he want me to make the money by going with
other men. Now I get so angry with him. I want to hurt him
back.

FR. FINEGAN
Have you no one to help you?

ANGELINA
No family here. Everybody in Old Country.

FR. FINEGAN
Then, as bad as he is, you can't leave him. Think of the disgrace of being, how do you say a divorced person in your language?

ANGELINA
*Una divorziata.*

FR. FINEGAN
Yes. You have to think of the children.

ANGELINA
He is touching them.

FR. FINEGAN
I don't understand.

ANGELINA
My oldest daughter, Raffaella. She is almost eleven. She tells me he is touching her like he should not.

FR. FINEGAN
You're sure of this? Children can be very imaginative. Or if he is drinking too much —

ANGELINA
He is touching her. And he looks at my second daughter.

## *Shift 47*

*The priest leaves while Woman #2 as her mother, Filumena, comes to stand behind Angelina who starts to write a letter.*

ANGELINA
Dear Mama, it is many years since I wrote you.

FILUMENA
I told you then: a charming drunk who would always smile at you.
*Mimicking Pietro.*
"Good evening, Signora Valletti. What lovely weather this evening."

ANGELINA
Things went well for us at first.

FILUMENA
But I tell you, Angelina: He has bad blood, that one. Look in his eyes. He'll beat you as soon as love you.

ANGELINA
Since we came to Canada, Pietro cannot find regular work.

FILUMENA
And what do we know of his family? He comes from no-where we know.

ANGELINA
We fight now almost every day.

FILUMENA
This one's too handsome. And too crazy.

ANGELINA
He hits me, even takes a knife against me.

FILUMENA
No land of his own. No money in the bank.

ANGELINA
I have no friends here. No one can help me.

**FILUMENA**
If you come back as a *divorziata,* we are all disgraced.

**ANGELINA**
Sometimes I am even afraid for the children.

**FILUMENA**
So don't come begging for help. You are as one dead to us.
*Woman #2 leaves abruptly. Angelina turns away in despair.
Man #1 as Pietro sits up, howling in the agony of a bad dream,
and repeating the same phrases again and again. Raffaella
runs to him as a little girl.*

## *Shift 48*

**PIETRO**
Aaah! *Il cavallo mangia, mangia il mio cervello.* [The horse eats
my brain out!]

**RAFFAELLA**
Papa, what's wrong?

**PIETRO**
*Gli uccelli mangiano i miei occhi, mi divorano.* [Birds pick out my
eyes. They're eating me up.]

**RAFFAELLA**
You're having a nightmare. Wake up, Papa.

**ANGELINA**
*Entering the scene.*
*Che successe?* [What's wrong?]

**RAFFAELLA**
Papa's sick again with his bad dreams.

**ANGELINA**
*Calmati.* [Be quiet.]

PIETRO
*Non posso dormire. Stanno mangiando il mio cervello.* [I can't sleep. They're eating my brains out.]

ANGELINA
*Queste sono pazzie della mente. Basta adesso.* [This is just craziness in your mind. Enough now.]

RAFFAELLA
Mama, he's all wet.

ANGELINA
He's sweating. He has fever.

RAFFAELLA
No, he's wet himself. Like a baby.

PIETRO
*Va via.* [Get out.]

ANGELINA
Get me sheets and a towel.

RAFFAELLA
Why did Papa make pee-pee like a baby?
    *Pietro howls in humiliated anger and tries to strike her. She runs away screaming, while Angelina holds him down.*

ANGELINA
*Basta. Non capisce.* [Enough. She doesn't understand.]

PIETRO
*È una puttana. Come voi.* [She's a whore like you.]

ANGELINA
I am no whore.

PIETRO
*Ah sì, sì!* [Oh, yes you are.] With this white man. With this Nish.

ANGELINA
*Sei veramente pazzo.* [You're really crazy.]

PIETRO
No, no. I no crazy. I see how you look at him.

ANGELINA
Because he is kind to us.

PIETRO
How much money he give you?

ANGELINA
Not a penny.

PIETRO
I tell you charge two, three dollars for each man. Five dollars if man stay all night. So how much you have made?

ANGELINA
Nothing. I touch no one.

PIETRO
*Slapping her.*
Bugiarda! [Liar!]

ANGELINA
Except Mr. Nish. And he only pay for room and board.

PIETRO
I swear I kill you. Then I kill him.
*He lets out a howl of anger. He strikes her again and again. She tries to fight back, and for a moment they struggle together. Pietro gets her in a headlock, hissing in her ear.*

PIETRO
I swear if you do not get me twenty or thirty dollars by tonight, I kill you. I give you lots of trouble, and make you go far away. But any place you go, I find you and kill you.

ANGELINA

I have no money at all. You know that.

PIETRO

I go out now. When I come back, if I find you in the house, I kill you, and that fucking baby in your stomach.

*Abruptly he leaves her. Lights fade down to a pinspot on a bewildered Amelia.*

## Shift 49

AMELIA

*Solo.*

"Shall I kill her, you want me to kill her?" Hughie holding Mama down, choking her. Like Pietro beating my grandmother. Bastards! Stinking of whiskey and sweat. Something in the blood. Deeper, some dark little gene that shapes your nose, and you inside. Did I get it from him or Angelina? No! Don't blame them. You're responsible for your own life.

*Beat.*

What a laugh. You just get on the streetcar and go for the ride: Angelina, and Mama, and me. "Shall I kill her, you want me to kill her?" Mama!

## Shift 50

AMELIA

Mama, please, what I'm trying to figure out is how all of these stories — I don't care how far back they go — all of them made me what I am today. And you too.

RAFFAELLA

Leave well enough alone, I say. Too much remembering and crying in this house.

AMELIA

Oh, Mama, I'm not saying it's your fault at all.

RAFFAELLA
Then why do I feel guilty?

TONI
Grandma, when you're the victim of abuse — especially as a kid — you feel responsible for everything. But it's not true. Please remember that.

RAFFAELLA
I used to wonder what did I do to make him touch me. I heard lots of stories like it. A father or uncle or family friend. You could be sitting on his knees — with people around you — and he'd have his hand up your dress.

TONI
Fuck him. Your own mother refused to believe you. That's what's awful.

RAFFAELLA
What was she supposed to do? No one talked about — no one admitted such things then.

AMELIA
If I had known this before —

RAFFAELLA
It wouldn't have done you a bit of good.

AMELIA
Possibly. Except when I look at you and Angelina, maybe I'm seeing myself.

RAFFAELLA
Why do you have to know everything?

AMELIA
Because I'm afraid it made me what I am today. Like I'm making up for someone else's crime, and I never knew she existed. You slapping me around because your own mother kicked you around.

**RAFFAELLA**

She was like him sometimes — half-crazy. Too many kids in the house and another on the way. Nagging at Papa, because there was no money coming in.

**AMELIA**

Which made you what you are, and what I am.

**TONI**

Let her alone.

**AMELIA**

Mind your own business.

**TONI**

This is family business. Do you know why I want to get out of this house? Because no one respects anyone! Especially me.

**AMELIA**

Shut up!

**TONI**

Right! Treat anyone like this and what do you expect?

**RAFFAELLA**

I'm going home. I'm tired of all the hollering and the bad memories.

**AMELIA**

Mama, you haven't finished the story.

**RAFFAELLA**

It's all there in your files.

**AMELIA**

No, it isn't. You're the only one left who was there that morning.

**RAFFAELLA**
I don't want to remember.

**AMELIA**
I'm asking you for help.

**RAFFAELLA**
If you knew how much it hurts to think about it.

**AMELIA**
I know, but it's important to know the truth — for all of us.

**RAFFAELLA**
You don't know when to stop, do you? It's enough to drive anyone crazy.

**AMELIA**
I swear I'll never ask you to do this again.

**RAFFAELLA**
Be careful what you ask for, my girl. Maybe you don't want to know everything.

**AMELIA**
Just this once. That's the bargain.

**RAFFAELLA**
*After a long, hard stare.*
All right. I'll tell you as much as I can.

## Shift 51

*Raffaella walks to the kitchen table to join Angelina and Pietro.*

**RAFFAELLA**
When we woke up Easter morning, we heard them fighting again. But Michele and Domenico were hungry so we went downstairs.

ANGELINA
*Briskly to the children.*
Quick, you eat breakfast. Then you get ready to go to mass with the Benedettis.
*Half-drunk, Pietro grabs Raffaella and pulls her toward him, trying to kiss her.*

PIETRO
*Da mi un piccolo baccio.* [Give me a little kiss.]

ANGELINA
Let her eat her breakfast.

PIETRO
*No, no. È una buona figlia.* [No, no. She's a good girl.]
*He is touching Raffaella. She pulls away. He slaps her.*
*Eh tu, piccola puttana!* [Hey you, little whore.]

ANGELINA
Why you hit her?

PIETRO
She's mine, so why not?
*To Raffaella.*
Hey, you gonna be a *puttana* like your mother? Except she do it for nothing. So maybe something bad happen to the bastard in her stomach.
*He pulls Raffaella back to him again. She resists, pulling away again.*

RAFFAELLA
Let me alone!

PIETRO
*Puttana! Troia!* [Whore! Bitch!]
*Pietro turns sharply and slaps her across the face. She screams in shock. This pushes Angelina over the edge. She shouts at the children.*

ANGELINA

All of you — go! Get dressed for mass.

PIETRO

*Shouting.*

Why you send them to church? Everybody see they dressed like beggars. Maybe I should take them away. Then you can raise your bastard all alone.

ANGELINA

*Porco miseria! Bruta bestia!*

> *Angelina erupts again, this time going after Pietro. He is sober and strong enough to struggle with her. Their fight is matched by a crescendo of dissonant sound that cuts off abruptly. Lights black out on them. A moment later a pinspot picks up Raffaella.*

## *Shift 52*

RAFFAELLA

We get dressed fast and I take the kids to the Benedettis. But I tell Mrs. Benedetti, "I gotta help Mama. She's not feeling so good."

> *Pointing to her stomach.*

I go back to the house. Because I saw the look on Mama's face, and I know something is wrong. But when I get there, they're not fighting any more. The house is quiet. I don't want to go in. It's a beautiful, warm day, so I sit by the back door instead. I can look in the kitchen window. Mama is sitting there so quiet. Staring straight ahead. As if she's thinking of something real hard. Finally she gets up and starts to walk upstairs. But why is she going upstairs with an axe? I come into the house. But quiet, so quiet, through the kitchen to the hallway, at the foot of the steps. I listen and listen, but I can't hear anything but the creak of the floor boards above me. A few minutes later, Mama comes down stairs, and I run outside.

*Pause.*

Except I could see there was blood on the axe she was
carrying. So I'm standing outside — as if I just got home —
when she comes to the door . . .

### ANGELINA
Raffaella, quick! Get your brothers and sisters.
*Raffaella exits for a moment. Angelina carefully hides the axe.
Lights crossfade back to the kitchen where she sits and beckons
the children to join her.*

### ANGELINA
All of you. Sit down. Now we must talk.

### RAFFAELLA
We're together for the last time, me and Amelia and Michele
and Domenico, except I didn't know it then.
*She walks into the scene with Angelina, as a child again.*

### RAFFAELLA
What's wrong, Mama?

### ANGELINA
Listen carefully. I have to go away for a while. But you will
not be alone. Soon you will have a new brother or sister. So
all of you must help Raffaella with the new baby.

### RAFFAELLA
Why do you have to go away?

### ANGELINA
I will write you, and you must write back every week to show
me how good is your English. So for a while we will be apart.
A long while maybe. Raffaella, you must promise Mama to
take care of all your brothers and sisters, the best way you
can, till I come back to you.

### RAFFAELLA
I promise, Mama. But where are you going?

*No answer from Angelina who leans back in her chair.*

ANGELINA

Now we can rest a while. I am tired. So warm for April here. But not like back home. Already there are fruit trees blooming in the orchard behind our house. Mama and me do the laundry, all the sheets like big white wings blowing in the wind . . .

RAFFAELLA

Is Easter a big holiday there too?

ANGELINA

Oh yes. And the whole week before. Like on Good Friday. First, we dress the statue of the Blessed Virgin, all in black. Jesus is dressed in black too, but in another church. Then at dawn on Easter, the bells ring from every steeple in town. The men carry Our Lady and Jesus. The sun is rising as the statues come toward each other through the streets of the town with the women and children singing. The bells get louder and louder as they come closer together in the great square. Jesus bows to Mary his Mother and she bows back with great respect. Then poof! The black robes are pulled off and underneath they are dressed all in white and gold. The children have white doves and now they let go of them. Hiy!

*With a sharp arm gesture up.*

So the sky is filled with white wings! And then fireworks start, all colors of the rainbow, louder and brighter, till you want to cry out . . .

*She laughs with Raffaella as they enjoy the image. Then Angelina starts to hum a song while she rocks back and forth. For a few moments Raffaella relaxes with her — perhaps even joining in the song — lost in the warm comfort of the afternoon and her mother's singing.*

RAFFAELLA

That was her last gift to us — that hour in the kitchen, talking about the new baby and singing, and just being quiet, our only heritage.

*Long pause.*

Then she got up to ask the Benedettis to call the police. When they came, she said . . .

ANGELINA

Here I am. Take me. I am ready to die.

## Shift 53

AMELIA

*Solo.*

Look in the mirror. There's the person you swore you'd never become. The mirror laughs: "See the crazy lady — funny nose — bad temper." Like Mama. Like Angelina? Oh Jesus Mary! A funny house of mirrors where you see yourself — worse and worse — endlessly. If you take one step, you fall down forever. And no one will let you get up.

*Pause.*

Stop. Go and find something real. Mama!

## Shift 54

AMELIA

Mama, what was it really like after they arrested Angelina? I have articles and pictures from the newspapers, but they can't tell the whole truth —

*She is interrupted by Man #2 who appears in a spotlight as Editor Curran of the Sault Ste. Marie newspaper, pompously editorializing. Behind him is Woman #2 as Anna Fishback.*

EDITOR CURRAN
*Overlapping her.*
From the Editor's Desk: Tuesday, May 2nd. Lest we see Angelina Napolitano only as a poor victim —

RAFFAELLA
*Overlapping him.*
They didn't let us read any newspapers.

EDITOR CURRAN
Let me point out that she pleaded for her husband's release last November —

RAFFAELLA
It was all lies and rumors.

EDITOR CURRAN
After he allegedly knifed her! In addition, I have it on highest authority that Angelina Napolitano had an adulterous affair with a Mr. Nish which created a public scandal. Then she nearly lost her children to the Children's Aid Society for neglecting and beating them.

RAFFAELLA
All lies! Where did they ever get those stories?

EDITOR CURRAN
And who shall repair the damage to our city's reputation when this scandal has provoked reaction around the globe? For instance, a reporter from *The Chicago Tribune* — an hysterical suffragette called Anna Fishback —

ANNA FISHBACK
The whole world is talking about Angelina Napolitano and her bravery. We have letters and petitions for her cause from around the globe: London-Vienna -Warsaw — even Australia. Reader, think of your mother — your wife —your daughter — and thank God the little woman had the courage of a tigress to slay the beast who threatened her honor.

EDITOR CURRAN
And all of this for a woman who comes from a people who
are — by nature — prone to violence. Italians follow the law
of the jungle. They use the knife — or axe — to redress any
wrong. So if we do not hang Mrs. Napolitano, her case
becomes a dangerous precedent.

TONI
You can't print that kind of crap!

AMELIA
Then you could. And worse. The question was: of what
value are these Italian immigrants?

EDITOR CURRAN
Italians are willing to perform brute labor for low wages. But,
at the same time, they are prone to drink — in addition to
being overly sexual — and highly excitable. Like most col-
ored peoples of Asia, Africa, the Mediterranean and the
South Americas — Jews included, of course. Italians are the
major source of intemperance, immorality and crime.

TONI
But you've got people writing in from all over the world to
save her.

AMELIA
And lots of media pressure from the Yanks.

EDITOR CURRAN
Why should we wish to emulate the example of the United
States? Of course, their newspapers — newsrags, I might say
— have instigated campaigns to save Mrs. Napolitano. But
this is from a country where women murder their husbands
in cold blood and then go scot-free.

TONI
*Basta!* I can't stand this prick.
*The spotlight on Curran and Anna goes out.*

**AMELIA**
You see, mama. The whole world knew about us. Much good all that lying did us. Did they let you see your mother in prison?

**RAFFAELLA**
Once or twice, just before she had the baby.

## Shift 55

*Angelina has been sewing baby clothes. She drops them and stares at Raffaella entering her cell. Neither one is sure what to say or do next. She embraces Raffaella fervently, then they stand back for a clumsy silence. Finally, Angelina speaks.*

**ANGELINA**
*Pointing to Raffaella.*
A new apron, yes?

**RAFFAELLA**
*As a child.*
Mrs. Walden made it for me.

**ANGELINA**
They are good to you at that house?

**RAFFAELLA**
It's all right. The boys miss you a lot.

**ANGELINA**
Yes. Me too. But soon they will have a new brother or sister.

**RAFFAELLA**
When, Mama?

**ANGELINA**
Before the end of this month. I been making a little . . .

*To Raffaella.*
*Come si chiama — una cammicia di notte?* [How do you say . . .
nightgown?]

RAFFAELLA
Nightgown, Mama. It's pretty.

ANGELINA
I thinking about name for the baby.

RAFFAELLA
I like Shirley.

ANGELINA
It will be Filumena. So you shouldn't forget your grandmother. I almost gave it to you.

RAFFAELLA
Oh, no!

ANGELINA
And if it's a boy, maybe you should ask Michele what he
would like his new brother to be called.

RAFFAELLA
I almost forgot! Michele wrote a letter to you. The lady from
Children's Aid helped him.
*Giving it to Angelina.*
She said they were going to put it in the newspaper. It's
pretty good. His teacher says his printing is very clear now.

ANGELINA
*Reading.*
"Dear Mama, I hope you will come to us soon. Raffaella takes
good care of us. So does Amelia sometimes. But we all want
you. We are lonesome every night without you."
*She is too close to tears to continue. Raffaella realizes this and
offers . . .*

RAFFAELLA

You want me to read it for you, Mama?

*Angelina nods and hands her the letter.*

"I go to school every day. I can write good now. Mrs. Walden lets us play in a big grassy yard where there are flowers. But we all want you to come home to us. Your loving son, Michele."

*Angelina puts a hand to her mouth to restrain her tears. She does not wish to weep in front of her daughter. She takes the letter, kisses it and puts it in her bosom. She is interrupted by Woman #2 as suffragist and reporter, Anna Fishback, a bustling woman of indomitable energy, who is followed by Man #2 as Charlie, a photographer carrying a camera on a tripod.*

ANNA FISHBACK

*Shouting from offstage.*

No, Ma'am, I'm not waiting another minute. Don't you dare try to keep me out. Bring your camera in, Charlie. Mrs. Napolitano, an honor to meet you.

*Shaking hands vigorously.*

Anna Fishback. On special assignment from *The Chicago Tribune*. We'd like an interview and a photo. Is this your little girl?

*Angelina nods, bewildered.*

Wonderful opportunity. What's your name, little girl? Charlie, tell me when you're set to go. Mrs. Napolitano, let me assure you that an interview — and photo — in *The Chicago Tribune* will give you millions of supporters.

*Pulling a document out of her purse.*

I already have a petition with 7,000 names for your minister of justice.

ANGELINA

*Ma che succede? Non capisco niente.* [What's going on? I don't understand anything.]

RAFFAELLA
*To Anna.*
Mama doesn't know what you're talking about.

ANNA FISHBACK
My God, have they been keeping this a secret from you, Mrs. Napolitano? The whole world is talking about you and your bravery. Everyone knows they're not going to hang you. The only question is how long they're going to keep you in jail. We want you out of here before your baby is born. What your lawyer could not accomplish, this petition — and dozens more like it from around the world — certainly will. Now, let's get this picture. Mrs. Napolitano, seated please. Little girl standing at her side. Arm around your mama, sweetheart. A brave smile. Wait! Charlie, give her the sewing. Let's see that lovely little nightdress. Now, big smile everyone.

*The light explosion of a camera and lights pop out on the scene. Pinspot on Amelia who talks to audience as she goes through box with research files and photos.*

## Shift 56

AMELIA
*Solo.*
Here are the children, staring stiff and puzzled, into the lens. Waiting for Angelina to come back. Petitions come from around the world. Anna Fishback keeps writing editorials. Until one day comes the reprieve — but not the pardon. Then the parole requests start. Three, five years, then seven years pass. Would her kids even recognize her now? "Not yet" say the authorities, "Too soon. Let her sit in jail a little longer to prove . . ." What? Eleven years! What do you accomplish by keeping her there? And what does she say when you visit her in prison, Mama?

ANGELINA
*Finger to lips.*
Shhh. Silence and shame. That is your heritage, Raffaella.

## *Shift 57*

*Lights crossfade to other half of the area as Amelia walks up to Angelina, holding the carton of research material. The other women pull down the Clytemnestra cape and form a circle with it.*

AMELIA
Looking for you, Angelina. If I find you — when I think I've got you . . .
*A pause as she waits for an answer from Angelina, which does not come. The rest of the women join her, so that eventually they form a group in a pool of light, wrapped in the Clytemnestra cape.*

RAFFAELLA
There comes a moment when you're beyond fear or panic. You go over the line, you fall into numbness, you only have to fall forward.

TONI AND RAFFAELLA
And everything else follows.

ANGELINA
Because if you kill him first, he can no longer hurt you. And there's no way to escape from him —

RAFFAELLA AND ANGELINA
Except by picking up the axe.

AMELIA
See — feel — the heft of the axe — strange in your hands — because you're not standing next to the woodpile . . .

AMELIA AND ANGELINA
But in your bedroom.

ANGELINA
Musty and stale, the air clogs your nostrils. On the bed he stirs . . .

ANGELINA AND RAFFAELLA
. . . Restless in his sleep as usual.

RAFFAELLA
A wave of his smell reaches you: sour sweat and liquor — the stench of his body that you have never grown used to.

ANGELINA
You hold your breath — as if even that sound might startle him. The room and everything in it seems to weigh upon you . . .

ANGELINA AND TONI
. . . Pushing itself against you, pushing you further.

TONI
And you know that when the afternoon sun disappears, he will wake as usual . . .

TONI AND RAFFAELLA
. . . And you will have missed your chance.

RAFFAELLA
You see yourself in the mirror for a moment, caught in the carved frame, the axe rising slowly . . .

RAFFAELLA AND ANGELINA
. . . Like a picture from some book.

ANGELINA
You can't breathe. You raise your arms to cut through the heat and stench of this hot afternoon. The air is as thick as

pig's blood. It makes you feel that you are drowning —
falling under waves of heat and stink and fear. . .

ANGELINA AND AMELIA
. . . Where you cannot breathe.

AMELIA
And the only way to push up and out of this whirlpool is to
raise the axe high above you and bring it down —

AMELIA AND RAFFAELLA
— Sharply on his skull!

RAFFAELLA
It's like splitting a melon open.

TONI
The sound surprises you. So you have to yank the axe high
and bring it down again —

TONI AND AMELIA
. . . And again!

AMELIA
No sound when you hit him. Except that his body twitches.
He gasps or moans, then another slight movement —

AMELIA AND ANGELINA
— And you hit him again.

ANGELINA
— Terrified that you may have only wounded him, and that
he will come after you.

AMELIA
But you go beyond the terror. Now comes the wave that
sweeps you on and on..

ANGELINA
Because now I know what it's like, when he hits me.

AMELIA
You want to taste the blood, feel it on your skin.

RAFFAELLA
If you can't give life, at least you can take it away.

ANGELINA
I want to split him open — spill him open —

AMELIA
. . . See the guts, the brains, the muscles that torture you.

RAFFAELLA
It's like the bells at mass, the choir singing.

ANGELINA
Better than making the baby in your belly.

AMELIA
Smashing the bone and cutting the muscle, is —

RAFFAELLA
— So simple and complete, because —

ANGELINA
— Even God cannot do more than this!

AMELIA
How can you tell when he's dead?

ANGELINA
You can't!

ALL THE WOMEN
*So keep hitting him!*

RAFFAELLA
No! I didn't mean to — I didn't, Mama. I swear.
*Suddenly they are all screaming and howling, moving in a frenetic choreography of chopping the body, as the amplified sound of an axe-fall distorts into a shattering crescendo.*

## Shift 58

*Raffaella is so hysterical that Toni and Amelia have to hold her.*

RAFFAELLA
All my fault. Forgive me, Mama. Everything destroyed, because of me.

AMELIA
Stop blaming yourself. How could a little girl destroy a family?
*Toni moves in to embrace Raffaella from behind, protecting her.*

RAFFAELLA
Don't want to talk about it anymore.

TONI
You want some camomile tea, Grandma?

RAFFAELLA
No. Need to get home. Have to be by myself.

AMELIA
You can't leave in this condition.

RAFFAELLA
I told you it was stupid to remember all this. Digging up all that guilt.

AMELIA
What are you talking about?

RAFFAELLA
I was there and — never mind. You got your bargain.

AMELIA
But you're not making any sense.

RAFFAELLA
I've said enough. Give me my coat.

AMELIA
Did something else happen after you went back to the house?

RAFFAELLA
Can't talk about it anymore.

AMELIA
*Realizing this is a critical moment.*
Mama, for chrissake, aren't you tired of carrying all this guilt and shame?

RAFFAELLA
It's all over, whatever happened.

AMELIA
There's no such thing as the past being over. It keeps happening again and again, right here and now.

TONI
Let her be.

AMELIA
Come on, Mama! The shape of my nose, the way I get angry, it's from you and Angelina.

RAFFAELLA
If you're going to blame me for everything that's happened . . .

TONI
Stop badgering her.

AMELIA
Will you fuck off and let her talk!

TONI
Why does she have to say anything? Angelina gets trapped with a bad husband, and so does Grandma and you. Notice

a pattern here? Well, I don't intend to get stuck in it. I'm not doing a repeat performance.
*Starting to leave.*

AMELIA
Where the hell are you going?

TONI
I'm moving in with Peter and Mark.

RAFFAELLA
My God, I'm watching this family fall apart in front of me.

TONI
I haven't got much choice, Grandma. This is survival.

RAFFAELLA
*Shouting.*
You goddam little fool. I've spent my life trying to keep my family together! Fifty years of working and slaving.

AMELIA
With how many secrets and lies?

RAFFAELLA
*Finally exploding as she gives up.*
All right! You want the whole story?

AMELIA
That was the bargain.

RAFFAELLA
You may be sorry you asked, my dear.
*Pause.*
I didn't go to the Benedettis that Easter morning. I waited on the front porch till I saw Mama going upstairs — carrying an axe. I follow her. Up, up the steps.

## *Shift 59*

RAFFAELLA

Quiet, careful, so Mama can't see me. Through the half-open door, I see Mama looking at Papa sleeping. The axe is next to her. Suddenly I know what she's going to do. And I want her to do it. I almost scream, "Stop!" But a part of me wants him to die, for all the fights, and his fingers poking me, pawing me. Mama raises the axe. I am happy and excited because . . . Mama hits him once! He moves a little. Twice! He makes a sound. Three times! His body twitches. He draws his knees up, like he's trying to pull himself into a ball.

*Pause.*

Then he's quiet. Mama drops the axe and turns her back on him. She thinks it's over. But I see his arm come up, reaching toward her. Or do I? I don't know anymore. I run into the room. Pick up the axe. Hit him on his head where he's bleeding, on his arm that he's stretching out toward us. Again and again.

*Screaming.*

Stop it! Don't ever touch me again. You hear? Never touch me again! Ahhhh.

*Howling, Raffaella raises her arms, the other women screaming with her. The impulse to axe Pietro has taken over her body as Angelina does the same movement. Amelia and Toni grab Raffaella; for a moment they are a cluster of three, fighting and embracing each other at the same time.*

RAFFAELLA

*Suddenly exhausted.*

Except I never told. That was the worst. I hope you're satisfied now. What are you going to do about it?

*A long silence. The women look at Raffaella who sits, trying to get her breath. Toni kneels next to her, as if to support her.*

## Shift 60

AMELIA
*Solo.*
Open the envelope. It comes spilling out — all the parts of you that were missing. Finally! The grandmother who had to pick up the axe. The grandfather who was crazy and drunk. My father who was worse than both of them. And me? I'm dragging the past behind me. Like a loaded sack I can't get rid of. Running in circles, repeating . . . No! Won't believe that. Oh please, help me smash through the door. Get out . . . out! Mama!

## Shift 61

AMELIA
Mama, there was one thing that the doctor and the coroner did agree on: Pietro was dead by the third blow at the latest.

TONI
You hear that, Grandma? You couldn't have been responsible for his death.

RAFFAELLA
Wouldn't have happened if I hadn't made a fuss, just kept my mouth shut.

TONI
It wasn't your fault — any of it.

RAFFAELLA
What do you know? I wanted him dead.

AMELIA
No. Listen: You were just a little girl — hysterical. The deathblow was the third one. Your mother killed him.

RAFFAELLA

But Mama did it to save me and Amelia and the baby inside her.

TONI

Then it was self-defense, Grandma. You were innocent.

RAFFAELLA

Don't tell me about innocent children. They can hate — want you dead — as much as any grown-up. Then I broke my promise to Mama. All she wanted was for us to stay together. The lawyers said it might take two, three years to get a pardon. But they separated us, wouldn't even tell me where the others were.

AMELIA

There was nothing a little girl could do about that.

RAFFAELLA

I'm not doing much better now, am I?

TONI

Grandma, it's not the same thing. You had a family then. I don't know where we are now — except falling apart.

RAFFAELLA

So I fail again! Something in our blood.

AMELIA

Jesus, Mary! Why is it so hard to give up guilt? Please, Mama. Let it go. And the shame with it. We've all dragged it around after us, like prisoners.

RAFFAELLA

I'm so tired. Remembering wears you out.

AMELIA

Another thing I don't understand. After she was released, why didn't your mother come back to you?

RAFFAELLA
It was thirteen years later. We all had separate lives.

TONI
But you saw your brother Michele.

RAFFAELLA
Not after he disappeared out west. Years later Domenico, the youngest, was killed in a construction accident. Then Amelia disappeared.

TONI
The baby who was born in prison.

RAFFAELLA
Filumena. She died about six weeks after she was born. I wasn't allowed to see her.
*This stops everyone for a moment. They are unsure how to comfort Raffaella. Amelia tries to embrace her, but Raffaella's stolid manner indicates she neither wants nor needs comfort at this moment.*

AMELIA
So your mother didn't stay in touch after they released her.

RAFFAELLA
Oh, she did.

## Shift 62

ANGELINA
If I come back, I ruin everything.

RAFFAELLA
There's plenty of jobs in North Bay, Mama. Or we could move somewhere else.

ANGELINA
Maybe something bad in our blood.

RAFFAELLA
I was in that room too.

ANGELINA
Shhh. Enough shame and dishonor.

RAFFAELLA
If we can find Michele and the others —

ANGELINA
You get married soon. Make a new life. You were always a good girl.

RAFFAELLA
*A howl.*
What good does it do me? Why did you kill him?

ANGELINA
If I have not done it, you would hate me. And because I do it, we lose each other.

RAFFAELLA
*The realization hits her.*
Oh Jesus, Jesus, Mary, you knew this would happen.

ANGELINA
What would you have done?

RAFFAELLA
I don't know.


*Shift 63*

AMELIA
Dear Lord, something is wrong here, when the only choice you have can destroy you.

TONI
What happened when she got out?

RAFFAELLA
She went to Montreal to look for Amelia. Then she disappeared too.

AMELIA
Waste. Oh Mama, too much waste.

TONI
So you were all alone.

RAFFAELLA
No, I did trace Michele to B.C. with his wife and kids.

AMELIA
We have family out there?

RAFFAELLA
Lots of cousins and your uncle.
*Ironic.*
Are you going to phone them now?

AMELIA
No, Mama. I just feel relieved. Getting through this is like —
*Groping for words.*

TONI
Going to the dentist!

AMELIA
No. More like an exorcism.

RAFFAELLA
I want to go home.

AMELIA
I'll drive you, Mama. But I have to call Elisabeth first. And talk to Vinny.

RAFFAELLA
Are you going to leave him?

AMELIA
He knows it's over.

RAFFAELLA
You could live in this house and just have nothing to do with each other. God knows how many people live like that.

AMELIA
Not me, Mama.

TONI
She's not going to walk out, Grandma. Too chicken.

RAFFAELLA
You divorce him, don't look for any help from me.

AMELIA
I think I've already left him. I just haven't said it out loud yet.
*Meanwhile Man #1 as Vinny has walked into Amelia's space. This time he is quiet but still angry.*

## *Shift 64*

VINNY
So you're gonna do it.

AMELIA
Elisabeth will talk to your lawyer.

VINNY
I get pushed out of my own home.

AMELIA
We can split it down the middle. Until we sell it.

VINNY
Yeah, yeah. Your bathroom, my bathroom.

AMELIA
Toni's leaving.

VINNY

To get away from your craziness.

AMELIA

I'm not the only one driving her out of this house.

VINNY

Where do you go then?

AMELIA

I don't know. Mama doesn't want me to move in with her.

VINNY

Do you know what the fuck you're doing at all?

AMELIA

I'm not really sure.

VINNY

So, twenty years, down the toilet.

*No response from Amelia spurs him on.*

I thought I married Miss Perfect. Pretty enough, and smart enough. You were too anxious, Sweetheart. Couldn't trust me or yourself. I was never good enough. Neither were you maybe.

*Exiting the stage.*

AMELIA

I'm sorry.

## Shift 65

TONI

I'm going to make tea. Grandma, you want some?

RAFFAELLA

No. I'm getting my coat and hat. And I have to go to the bathroom.

*Exits.*

TONI
Tea, Mama?

AMELIA
Yes, but hold on a moment.
*Phone rings.*
Elisabeth?

ELISABETH
How's it going, Sweetie?

AMELIA
Amazing! It's quite a story. Listen, I want to apologize for this afternoon —

ELISABETH
No need. Did you find out what you needed?

AMELIA
Oh yes. And more. Can you come over tomorrow? It's too much to tell on the phone. And I have something to do now, I'm ready to do now.

ELISABETH
I'll bring lunch. And we can put our feet up.

AMELIA
Thank you, yes.

ELISABETH
Try to get a good night's rest. Love you all.

AMELIA
Good night.
*Hanging up and turning to Toni.*
Are you still moving out?

TONI
*Nodding.*
You don't need me right next to you, Ma.

AMELIA
I'm tired of this war.

TONI
I didn't start it.

AMELIA
You are so strong and independent. You're terrifying.

TONI
I'll be back for dinner on Sunday. Are you going to see Don
again?

AMELIA
I don't know. I don't think I'm ready for anyone yet.

TONI
As far as men go, you're not going to do much better. And
he's cool enough to put up with your craziness.

AMELIA
*Defensive sarcasm.*
Thank you for the advice. Anything else?

TONI
*Indicating the room decor.*
Get rid of all this crap.

AMELIA
I spent good money for all these —

TONI
*Cutting her off.*
It's still crap. Except the music. Love that Bocelli.
*Amelia is breath-taken for a moment. Then she looks around
the chaotic room and reflects.*

AMELIA
Well, it is kind of bric-à-brac.

TONI
Ma, it's tacky!

AMELIA
Maybe Villa Colombo could use it.

TONI
They would love it.

AMELIA
*Agreeing with arms outstretched.*
Yes! I need more space! Give me music!

TONI
*Switching on the music.*
And I'll brew us a big pot of camomille.
*Woman #2 and Man #2 exit, as does Toni to the kitchen.*
*Lights crossfade to a pinspot on Amelia.*

## Shift 66

AMELIA
*Solo.*
Open a closet door and all kinds of skeletons come tumbling out. No, not skeletons. All those beautiful household saints you want to revere: Grandma and Grandpa, stiff and formal in their wedding finery. Except he was a psycho and she was a murderess. But you still want to light the candles. Even if you don't repeat the history. After all, they are your family. Their blood made you — keeps running through your veins. Look in the mirror and see the same eyes, same nose, same craziness. Doesn't matter. You have to burn those candles — even knowing that you're closer to evil than you ever thought. Anyway, they didn't ask to be the family saints. They just wanted a good life for all of us. Murderers and *divorziate* included.

## Shift 67

*Bocelli singing "Con te partirò" comes up loud and clear on the soundtrack. Raffaella enters, putting on her coat and hat. Toni enters with a backpack, an armful of music scores, that she starts to pack.*

AMELIA

Oh Mama, no more secrets and lies. Doesn't it feel wonderful?

RAFFAELLA

Little girl, you are what you are after sixty years. The truth doesn't make you a different person. Not at my age anyway.

AMELIA

You know, Mama — you are not easy to live with.

RAFFAELLA

Neither are you, my dear.

AMELIA

I'm going ahead with the divorce, Mama.

RAFFAELLA

What's going to become of you?

AMELIA

I don't know. But I'm not asking for your blessing. I'll have to do it on my own.

RAFFAELLA

*After a long look.*

Just do your best.

> *Raffaella makes no further comment but starts to pin her hat on. Amelia is captivated by the music. She allows it to take her over, half-dancing to it as she looks at Angelina.*

AMELIA
*Shouting over the music.*
Mama, I want to go to Easter vigil this year.

RAFFAELLA
Since when do you go to church?

AMELIA
I like the music.

RAFFAELLA
I've got work to do. Dinner for thirty people at least.

AMELIA
How do you feel about having a *divorziata* to Easter dinner?

RAFFAELLA
I'll see you on Sunday.
*Raffaella — complete with hat, coat and handbag — starts to leave. For a moment her eyes follow Angelina who is back in her upstage position where we saw her at the opening of the play, wrapped in her cape as Clytemnestra.*

CLYTEMNESTRA
Enough of killing!
We have reaped a harvest enough of death. We need
No more blood. What's done is done, and must be lived with.
I am a woman among men: but listen to me!
We have had enough death. Reason calls a truce at last.
*Raffaella halts abruptly and turns back to stare at Amelia.*

AMELIA
What's wrong, Mama?

RAFFAELLA
Well, the thing is: Would you have done it different? Or any better?

**AMELIA**
I don't know, Mama. I don't think so. I don't really know.
*Suddenly she is overtaken by an impulse that is somewhere between crying and hysterical laughter. Or is it just relief? She gives in to it, while Raffaella stares at her for a moment, but even she starts to laugh. Then Toni and Angelina laugh with them. The music increases in volume. Angelina lets her cape unravel so Amelia can wrap it around herself. She starts to pull herself toward her grandmother. As they approach each other, the music crescendoes and lights fade out.*

End of Play

# PRODUCTION NOTES

## *The Angelina Project*

*Transformations:* The script is written as a series of stories discovered and memories relived. A scene that is a flashback in history or a remembered recent event can, in turn, flow back to another moment. Indeed, it might be better not to think of this as a play with "flashbacks" to the past at all. Rather, think of time as fluid and parallel; the past keeps flowing through the present as a parallel stream. In addition, most of the actors can transform from one character to another as need be, so that time and space are instantly erased.

*Time and Place:* In place of detailed stage directions between scenes, I have used the term *shift* to indicate a change in time, place or reality. Both in reading or performance, there should be no pause here. Lights and sound should help to "gear-shift" the new scene into place.

*Setting:* A flat, neutral space. Several revolving stools or chairs strategically placed so that each actor can move in and out of a scene in a split second by angling the body or standing up. The only definable scenic elements are two "work stations" which are wheeled on early in the show. The first is Amelia's littered computer desk, while the second is Raffaella's kitchen table where she and Angelina work through much of the play.

*Accents:* Phrases in Italian are translated and follow the Italian phrase. Accent for any character should be minimal and suggestive. Perhaps Angelina's accent is a matter of a self-conscious slowness and deliberation when she is speaking English.

*Note:* The original source for this script was the article "Murder, Womanly Virtue, and Motherhood: The Case of Angelina Napolitano, 1911-1922" by Karen Dubinsky and Franca Iacovetta, in *The Canadian Historical Review,* Vol. LXXII, No. 4, December 1991.

# Acknowledgments

Thanks to Franca Iacovetta and Karen Dubinsky for the source article which inspired this script; Diane Quinn of Théâtre Nouveau who commissioned the script; Virginia Reh of Script Lab and especially Elise Dewsberry, dramaturge, who was invaluable in our 1998 workshop; Toronto Arts Council for two grants to write and workshop the text; WIFT-Toronto, Théâtre Passe Muraille [Jacoba Knaapen], Pacun Peras Theatre [Mario Tenorio] and Ontario Workers Arts & Heritage Centre [Renee Johnston] who sponsored readings of the play.